To Serve with Love

Also by Carnie Wilson

Gut Feelings: *From Fear and Despair to Health and Hope* (with Spotlight Health)

I'm Stili Hungry: *Finding Myself Through Thick and Thin* (with Cindy Pearlman)

Hay House Titles of Related Interest

Books

Eating in the Light: *Making the Switch to Vegetarianism on Your Spiritual Path,*
by Doreen Virtue, Ph.D., and Becky Prelitz, M.F.T., R.D.

Shape® Magazine's Shape Your Life: *4 Weeks to a Better Body—and a Better Life,*
by Barbara Harris, with Angela Hynes

The Truth: *The Only Fitness Book You'll Ever Need,* by Frank Sepe

Vegetarian Meals for People-on-the-Go, by Vimala Rodgers

A Very Hungry Girl: *How I Filled Up on Life . . .
and How You Can, Too!* by Jessica Weiner

The Yo-Yo Diet Syndrome: *How to Heal and Stabilize
Your Appetite and Weight,* by Doreen Virtue, Ph.D.

Card Decks

Healthy Body Cards, by Louise L. Hay

Juicy Living Cards, by SARK

Self-Care Cards, by Cheryl Richardson

All of the above are available at your local bookstore,
or may be ordered by visiting:

Hay House USA: **www.hayhouse.com**
Hay House Australia: **www.hayhouse.com.au**
Hay House UK: **www.hayhouse.co.uk**
Hay House South Africa: **orders@psdprom.co.za**

To Serve with Love

Simple, Scrumptious Dishes from the Skinny to the Sinful

Carnie Wilson

with

Cindy Pearlman

HAY HOUSE, INC.
Carlsbad, California
London •Sydney •Johannesburg
Vancouver •Hong Kong

Published and distributed in the United States by: Hay House, Inc., P.O. Box 5100, Carlsbad, CA 92018-5100 • *Phone:* (760) 431-7695 or (800) 654-5126 • *Fax:* (760) 431-6948 or (800) 650-5115 •www.hayhouse.com • ***Published and distributed in Australia by:*** Hay House Australia Pty. Ltd., 18/36 Ralph St., Alexandria NSW 2015 • *Phone:* 612-9669-4299 • *Fax:* 612-9669-4144 •www.hayhouse.com.au • ***Published and distributed in the United Kingdom by:*** Hay House UK, Ltd. •Unit 62, Canalot Studios •222 Kensal Rd., London W10 5BN • *Phone:* 44-20-8962-1230 • *Fax:* 44-20-8962-1239 •www.hayhouse.co.uk • ***Published and distributed in the Republic of South Africa by:*** Hay House SA (Pty), Ltd., P.O. Box 990, Witkoppen 2068 • *Phone/Fax:* 27-11-706-6612 •orders@psdprom.co.za • ***Distributed in Canada by:*** Raincoast •9050 Shaughnessy St., Vancouver, B.C. V6P 6E5 • *Phone:* (604) 323-7100 • *Fax:* (604) 323-2600

Editorial supervision: Jill Kramer   *Design:* Julie Davison   *Interior photos:* Martin Mann

The authors of this book do not dispense medical advice or prescribe the use of any technique as a form of treatment for physical or medical problems without the advice of a physician, either directly or indirectly. The intent of the authors is only to offer information of a general nature to help you in your quest for emotional and spiritual well-being. In the event you use any of the information in this book for yourself, which is your constitutional right, the authors and the publisher assume no responsibility for your actions.

Library of Congress Cataloging-in-Publication Data

Wilson, Carnie, 1968-
To serve with love : Simple, scrumptious dishes from the skinny to the sinful / Carnie Wilson with Cindy Pearlman.
p. cm.
ISBN 1-4019-0602-8 (tradepaper)
1. Cookery. 2. Low-calorie diet--Recipes. I. Pearlman, Cindy, 1964- II. Title.
TX714.W5254 2004
641.5--dc22   2004010542

ISBN 13: 978-1-4019-0602-3
ISBN 10: 1-4019-0602-8

08 07 06 05   4 3 2 1
1st printing, August 2005

Printed in Thailand by Imago

This book is dedicated to my Grandma Mae . . .
my first memories in the kitchen are with you.
No one loved, laughed, cared, worried,
or cooked like you. I love and miss you so much.

Also dedicated to my mother, Marilyn, and
my father, Brian. You gave me life, and
therefore you are my life. I love you both.

Contents

INTRODUCTION

To Serve with Love

A woman never forgets her first time, especially when her teacher is an expert with a loving touch. *In my case, it happened in 1979, on the brown-checked linoleum of my grandma's kitchen in West Hollywood. Even all these years later, I can still remember these whispered words: "Carnie, you must wait, dear. If you eat them now, you're going to get sick . . ."*

Hey, what are you thinking? This is my first cookbook, and I'm talking about my Jewish Grandma Mae, whom I've dedicated this book to because she was my ultimate favorite cook. Grandma was short and pudgy, with a cute round face that held no teeth (I swear to God). She had a fantastic sense of humor and a contagious laugh, and she was also the one who taught me the most important facts of life, including (of course) how to make her world-famous matzo balls.

As with other things that I'd discover for the first time later on, I learned that I needed to practice, practice, practice in order to *really* cook.

LET ME TELL YOU, PEOPLE, MY GRANDMA MAE SERVED. With love. It was her way, and it's the best way of all. Of course, she'd also hover over my beloved grandfather Irv and argue with him in Yiddish.

"What do you want from me, Mae?"

"Nothing! Just eat."

"I already ate!"

"That was ten minutes ago!"

While this went on, I'd sneak away to their pantry. This was my hideout, a place where I could eat half a bag of chocolate chips while contemplating the other things that were going on in my life: Why was I failing math? Why didn't that cute boy Ryan ask me to go steady with him? Why was I the fattest kid in my class?

When Grandma smelled that something was up, she'd whip open the pantry door. *Busted!* She'd put her hands on her round hips, and in a mock mad voice treat this like a police raid. "Please put those chips down, Carnie. Those are for my cookies!" she'd say, trying to look tough, but it never really came off that way.

To make her happy, I'd put the bag down and stick my hands up. And then I'd throw myself on the mercy of the court: "Sorry, Grandma. I will never, ever do it again. I promise." But when she'd turn her back, I'd eat six more chips and then put that sacred bag back on the shelf with a frown on my face.

Yes, I gave up the goods for a simple reason: There was actually one thing I liked better than eating in my preteen years. That was watching my grandmother in her adorable flowered, crisp-linen apron moving confidently around the kitchen. By the way, that room was her pride and joy after my parents remodeled it for her as a present. Now I know why I'm the way I am in the kitchen (look out, dirt!). My grandmother had stainless-steel sinks that she kept spotless and dry, wiping them down at least 100 times a day.

"I see a few spots, dear," she'd tell me. "Remember to wipe the sink after you run the water." Before I could even do a half-eye roll, I was humbled by the facts of kitchen life. "I love you, my *shana punim.* Just stay close to me and watch. Grandma will teach you," she'd say. It was good advice, and so very true.

As for Grandma Mae's cooking, no one dared question how anything tasted because it was all amazingly good: the five-pound matzo balls; the cinnamon-noodle kugel with crispy, slightly burned raisins on top; and the brisket covered with tangy, sweet onions that sizzled when they came out of the oven. And forget about her cheese soufflé, which I'd beg her over and over to make. Heaven! (I'll tell you about it later.) The bottom line was that if you were coming over to my grandparents' house, you were staying for dinner. The first question both of them would ask as you barely put a foot in the door was: "Are you hungry? What do you want to eat?"

Even after dinner, the same question was asked. They just really loved to feed people.

The only thing I never understood was the gefilte fish my grandparents ate with big smiles on their faces. There was a traumatic moment once when I bit into what I thought was a matzo ball (it was light and round and mushy), and it turned out to be gefilte hell. *Eww, yuck, gross!* I'll never like gefilte fish even though Grandma and Grandpa (the only ones at the table who actually ate it) would always shout out, "No, it's delicious! Try some." (No thanks!)

I can still fondly remember how my grandma chewed with no teeth and with her cheeks almost touching her eyelids with every bite. Darn, she was the cutest thing.

Now it dawns on me that the memories we all have of eating with our families and the people we love aren't really about the food at all. It's about sharing the joy of being together, the combined flavors of everyone's personality, and the full feeling of being a family. To see the smile on my grandmother's face, knowing that she made another great meal, made me feel as warm as her chicken soup. Those lazy childhood days in Grandma Mae's kitchen started a lifelong devotion. I knew that someday I'd also serve my family and friends. With love.

NOW A DISCLAIMER: Just because I had gastric-bypass surgery and lost 150 pounds doesn't mean that I don't love food or that I'm not able to enjoy a great meal. I never feel deprived. I mean, do you think that I'd ever give up the joy of cooking or eating? No freakin' way! I'll just serve a full plate to you and a half plate to me . . . which brings me to this book.

Over the years, many friends have called to ask, "Carn, can I borrow your black pumps? Oh, and why don't you write a cookbook? That was a really awesome dinner you made the other night—better than a restaurant." I'd hang up the phone, grab the shoes, and then stick my own toes into the kitchen to try out a few new recipes. I'd write down the good ones and pour the coffee grounds over the not-so-hot ones, all the while mentally promising that I'd put all the recipes together one day.

Even after I had my gastric-bypass surgery, I was determined to make food a beautiful thing in my life. At the time when I could only eat a few ounces of salmon every night, I made sure that mine was drizzled with just a splash of extra-virgin olive oil, balsamic vinegar, tomatoes, basil, and garlic. It made the food special. It made it appetizing. And it made it beautiful.

By the way, I lost all that weight by embracing real food, not by pushing it away. I just finally started paying attention to what I was putting in my mouth and really enjoying and appreciating good, healthy food for the first time.

The great news is that I now have some self-control (well, most of the time . . . a bite of chocolate is awfully hard to pass up), so I can make all the wonderful recipes in the world. Yet whether or not you've had surgery, I don't think there's any room in this life for deprivation when it comes to food. It's about portion control, not penalizing yourself with tasteless and bland "diet" foods.

Of course, there will always be some annoyingly skinny person in the room (you know who you are) who complains about being a double size zero, down from a horrifying size four when she let herself go that one week in 1998. This person will try to explain her love of a macrobiotic diet that consists mostly of beans, onions, and rice—meanwhile, I can only think one thing: *Hello, Gas-X!* Don't worry, you're not going to find any of those recipes here!

When I was fat, I ate fast food all the time—sometimes three times a day—and my life consisted of sugar and fried foods. Now you *will* find sugar in this cookbook, but you won't find one fried food here. Yes, it's true, I have a fear of frying because it doesn't make me feel good anymore, so I avoid it completely. For all you "normal tummy" folks, something doesn't need to be oil city in order to taste great. The truth of the matter is that when you cook at home, you can make dishes that are a lot cleaner—in other words, you know what's in there and what's not. If I want my food to drip with cheese, I can ensure that it's low-fat Swiss or mozzarella.

Speaking of dripping cheese, let's talk about enchiladas for a second. The ones you'll find in this book are so good that you won't even think of uttering that four-letter word: *diet.* I usually do a little salsa dance around the kitchen with my husband, Rob, after eating them. And he generally does something so magical and exciting that I can barely write the next few words. *He does the dishes. ¡Olé!* This is otherwise known as the age-old slogan: "I cook, you clean." (He's a good boy.)

OKAY, LET'S DISH ABOUT THIS BOOK for a moment. If it were a recipe, it would go something like this: Start with simple, tantalizing, scrumptious appetizers and party foods, easy breakfasts and brunches, satisfying lunches, and delicious dinners. Stir in dreamy desserts and scrumptious sides. (Do we really want anything else?) Add a generous helping of just plain fun and combine with enough tips that will convince anyone, including yourself, that you know your way around a kitchen. You'll make others smack their lips and ask for seconds. And you'll also hear these words: "Did you really make this yourself? Come on!"

I decided to write this cookbook for everyone who spent the better part of their 20s and 30s working their butts off, looking for love and hopefully finding it, and still working—to pay for the houses, the cars, and those high-priced designer shoes, which, incidentally, is all I loved when I was a size 28. (My shoe size was still a 9, which technically made my feet one of the smallest parts of my bod.)

The point is that we're not the generation that asked our mothers for cooking lessons. Maybe becoming a homebody never even crossed your mind. (I, for one, used to have no time at all for cooking.) But you don't have to be Susie Homemaker to learn how to cook. You might just discover that it relaxes you and makes you feel comforted and happy, like it does for me.

And don't even get me started when it comes to my obsession with cookbooks. (I own more than 500 of them, which are proudly displayed in my kitchen as tools and moral support.) I also know that I'm not the only one who relishes a day in bed watching hours of cooking shows. Paula Deen's desserts and twice-baked stuffed potatoes have soothed my sniffles. Even when I was trying to sweat out a cold in bed, Martha Stewart gave me the hope that tomorrow would be a better day—especially if I roasted some garlic and smooshed it into some mashed potatoes. (Now *that's* good medicine!) However, I also felt truly nauseated after watching her do everything so perfectly. I could never milk a wild yak. I mean, yaks are scary.

Now let's turn up the heat. From cooking, I get a sense of satisfaction, nurturing, comfort, and pride. You don't have to be successful in business or be a top actress or fashion model to be a great cook. *Anyone can do it.* There's nothing like knowing that you made a dish that's incredible.

Not long ago I was in the studio recording the new Wilson Phillips album (our first in 12 years—yeah!). I was talking up a few of the recipes for this book with the intensity of a woman discussing her new lover (believe me, if I could make love to my peach cobbler, I would), when our producer, Peter Asher, said, "Carn, I've never heard anybody talk about food the way you do. You certainly have a passion for cooking."

Passion, smashion! The bottom line is I love food intensely. Eating is still *it* for me in terms of what the most pleasurable feeling in the world is. It's an excitement, a thrill, a sensory sundae. Yes, I'm still obsessed with food, but just in a much healthier way now.

It made sense to me that I was talking recipes while recording the album. Food is like music to me: It makes my heart race.

People have to eat to live. I still live to eat. So sue me.

Of course, none of this dawned on me when I made cooking a part of my life ten years ago as a way to burn off stress. Somewhere along the way, I realized that just like painting or singing, cooking is also a lost art. But what is art unless you share it with others?

Back then I didn't share enough. The problem was that I was eating portions as big as a serving dish (and sometimes two), while now I might not finish a salad plate's worth. Art to me back then was a huge plate of pasta accented with cream sauce. Now I live with a much prettier picture: My main canvas is protein and veggies, but I add a few strokes of mashed potatoes, mac and cheese, or a fabulous casserole. That's a beautiful way to live.

This brings me to why I didn't do some bland, low-cal cookbook. Isn't that what you would have expected me to do? Well, I'm just not that gal. I eat *healthfully*—more clean food and less of the bad stuff. Believe me, I know that the bad food tastes the best. But guess what, everybody? I know a secret: *You can eat whatever you want. It's all about portion size.*

Life is too short to deny yourself anything, so I've dared to include the foods here that made me fat in the first place. But, you see, I got fat because I was out of control. Now I eat whatever I want, but I love and savor it, and I'm able to stay at a normal weight by watching how much of each food I eat. I also exercise regularly and drink a ton of water. It's truly the best of all worlds, and God knows I'm so grateful that I can live this way.

Of course, like most of you, I always want more. Sorry, everybody . . . there's no recipe for willpower. You've just gotta dig it up for yourself. But do it—it's so worth it.

So, what will I serve up in this cookbook?

This isn't one of those collections where you'll find fancy rabbit stew (God help me, I'd never cook a bunny!), nor is there anything that requires four days of prep. I don't know about you, but I'm a meat-and-potatoes girl. I wasn't raised on foie gras or venison fillets. I'll take a thick steak, mashed potatoes, and a Caesar salad over anything.

This is a book for you and your family. I don't want you to be intimidated by the recipes, but proud of them. Basically, I'll share what I know and love in this book, but I didn't want to pass on the information to you in a typical way. After all, cooking and eating isn't just about the food: Sometimes a beautiful centerpiece will make the meal so much more elegant or exciting, and there's nothing like great music playing to add to it. And simple things like candles and place mats can make it seem like you toiled for hours and hours.

In each chapter, I'll give you lots of tips and asides (which I call "Carnie Aside-a"s) so you don't get burned in the kitchen (although everyone has to step into the fire once or twice!). When it's time to cook, I'll give you the instruction and motivation to "Hit It" (watch for some fun and helpful tips here). I'll also help you get through what I like to call "butterfly-causing situations" that require food: You're making your significant other dinner for the first time, your judgmental mother-in-law is coming over, or you're having your friends over for the perfect "girls' night in." You *can* be the perfect hostess, I guarantee it.

But back to this book.

Some of the recipes included here have a higher-caloric version (which I call "The Sinful") and a healthier alternative (called "The Skinny"), so people on all sorts of eating plans will be satisfied. I know how to cook in ways that are light *and* right. You really can have low-carb and low-fat dishes without sacrificing one hint of taste. And while some recipes are labeled "Skinny," others aren't because they're skinny on their own.

I'm not an advocate of skipping dessert. Forget about it—that's the best part! So I'll show you how to make a cheesecake with a fat-free brownie mix and one percent milk. (Hang on a second . . . I have to take a deep breath just thinking about these desserts, because my upper lip has broken into a sweat.) As far as dinner for one goes, you're not taking it out of a box anymore. How do you think I started practicing when it came to cooking? I was my own captive audience. And I'm still alive! Who knew? Ha ha!

These days when I cook, I'm happiest when I see my husband smile and say, "Mmm, that's good. Thank you so much." I'm just like my Grandma Mae in that I love to feed people. I love it when my friends whisper, "Hey, Carn, you gotta give me that recipe." In fact, when I hear those words, I do a little silent flip inside. At such moments, I'm so happy, I could even eat a bite of gefilte fish. That is, I would if those grainy little fish balls still didn't make my brain scream, *Eww!*

Sorry, Grandma, but I'll take your matzo balls any day.

CHAPTER ONE

Talking the Talk

We've all thumbed through various cookbooks that start with a list of acceptable culinary terms. Blah, blah, blah. Boring, boring, boring. In my book, I'm going to look at these words in a bit of a different light.

Let's start with a few that are commonly misunderstood:

FRY/ SAUTÉ/POACH

Fry: The ultimate in naughty, delicious food prep, and most people's fave, but also known as "artery hell." This is what we secretly want to do with all food, but we know we can't or we'll weigh 400 pounds. (It's one of the ways I got to 300!) We won't do any of it in this book. When you fry, you're just asking for heartburn—keep reminding yourself of that fact.

Sauté: As close as you can get to frying, but you're still able to feel good about yourself. This is usually done when something is cooked in a small amount of oil or butter because it's actually good for you. I use olive oil about 99 percent of the time, but canola oil comes in a close second. Keep in mind the following:

- **Good Oils** include the omega-3s (such as what's found in salmon), or any olive oil—these are all actually great for your heart. When you don't have olive oil, canola is a nice alternative.

- **Bad Oils:** The kind you'd find in a Big Mac or Snickers. As for vegetable oil, try to avoid it.

Poach: Not as boring as it sounds, I promise. Basically, you're steaming food without losing the nutrients. Gosh, my mom would be so proud.

DASH/PINCH/SPLASH/DOLLOP

Dash: It's not half the bag of sugar; it's less than half a teaspoon. (Sorry to bum you out like this.) The other night in the kitchen, I actually found myself adding just a dash of chocolate shavings to a dish, instead of a mound the size of Mount Everest. If that ain't restraint, then I don't know what is. The honest truth is that too much is sometimes. . . . too much.

Pinch: What you want your significant other to do when he swings by the kitchen and catches you cooking. Okay, using a practical example: Much like a dash, you can stay pinch-worthy by just adding *a bit* of an ingredient to a recipe.

Splash: It's the same thing as a dash or a pinch, but in liquid form. It's like a drip—not the entire bottle—of maple syrup.

Dollop: A big hearty spoonful that you plop down like whipped cream over apple pie. By the way, you need to use a regular spoon here, not a garden shovel.

DICE/CHOP/JULIENNE

Chop: What I want to do to my inner thighs. . . . Here, it means to cut roughly.

Dice: When not in Vegas, it's to cut evenly into cubes of consistent size, usually about ¼"–½" inch.

Julienne: This means to cut into matchsticks, like shoestring potatoes. You can julienne in all different sizes.

Mince: A very fine chop. I won't mince words with this next comment: Just watch your fingers.

MARINATE/RUB/DEGLAZE/FOLD

Marinate: What I'd like to do is marinate myself in hot fudge. . . . When it comes to food, it's a way of tenderizing meat or soaking something to add flavor. Most marinades have an acid or enzyme that tenderizes, such as a citrus juice or vinegar.

Rub: What I ask my husband, Rob, to do to my feet, and it annoys him to no end. As far as food goes, this means to massage fresh herbs or other spices into a meat before cooking.

Deglaze: What I have to do to my eyes after watching another boring special on Britney Spears or J. Lo. In cooking, it means to add liquid to a pan and scrape up the bits until all the good stuff is blended together in your new juice.

Fold: This means to gently combine a light, airy mixture such as beaten egg whites or applesauce with a heavier mixture like custard or whipped cream. When you fold, start at the back of the bowl, using a rubber spatula to cut down vertically through the two mixtures, across the bottom of the bowl and up the nearest side. Rotate the bowl a quarter of a turn, repeating strokes. This turns the mixtures gently over the top of each other to combine, as opposed to just mixing or stirring together.

A FEW NEW TERMS

Slurry: It's not what happens to your words when you've had too many glasses of wine. It's actually a mixture of water, and a thickener such as flour or cornstarch. It's typical to add a slurry to pan drippings to make gravy, but you can actually add a slurry to any wet preparation in order to thicken it.

Chiffonade: This isn't that new skirt style that's "in"—it's actually a way to cut things, usually leafy ingredients like herbs. But first you roll them into long, thin strands. For example: Take basil leaves, stack them, and roll them into a cigar shape, then cut through it horizontally. Voilà! Basil chiffonade!

Macerate: This means to soak in liquid to cause food to soften or soak up a flavor. For instance, you macerate fruit in liquor sometimes. (Use this word on someone today; they'll be slightly impressed.)

Gene: This is my abbreviation for *genius*. The brownie recipe in this book? It's gene. The Eagles? Gene. Reuniting with Wilson Phillips is, of course, gene. My makeup artist's new Chanel lip gloss is gene, but my mom's sweet-potato casserole at Thanksgiving is beyond gene.

OKAY, NOW THAT WE'VE GOT all the lingo taken care of, we're just about ready to get started. But before we do, I want you to memorize the following six steps—post them on your fridge if you have to:

MY COOKING MANTRA

1. **Don't freak out.** Take a deep breath. It's gonna be fine. What's the worst thing that can happen: You burn the house down and have to move? You poison your guests? Seriously, when it comes to cooking, there absolutely are "do overs"—you try it and if it doesn't work, you start again tomorrow. See, no pressure. Know that you're going to knock your guests out with the food that you've cooked yourself, which is the best food of all.

2. Make sure to read a recipe in its entirety before you start. Cooking is not the time to welcome last-minute surprises, or you could wind up in the Land of Disaster.

3. **Make sure that you really do have all the ingredients** for the recipe—in fact, lay them out in front of you before you start. This ensures that you won't have to get in the car and go back to the store, which is always a huge pain.

4. **Yes, you really do have to measure ingredients out** instead of just "eyeballing" it. I know your granny cooked by an "eyeful" or by measuring flour in her favorite coffee cup. The only difference between our generation and hers is that we don't

own those same coffee mugs, and most of us wear contacts. In other words, our eyes aren't registered measuring devices. Trust me. Get yourself a good measuring set, including cups and spoons. If you have old crusty ones in the back of your cabinet, great (but wash 'em first, please).

5. **Now let's consider a new word** when it comes to being in the kitchen: *flow*. Recipes have a flow that's sort of like a dance. When you're making a meal, you need to know that when your meat is busy marinating, you can be cutting veggies to steam. But you can't put those asparagus stalks in the steamer until 15 minutes before serving time or you'll cook the life out of them. Oh, I should mention right now that the entire meal has a flow. Soon you'll be going with that flow, and all will make sense. Timing is the key to all recipes. Read Step 2 again—check each recipe for prep time.

6. **If all else fails, resort to prayer** . . . it never hurts. Also, trust yourself and learn from your mistakes. Try again. It takes time to learn how to cook, and everybody screws up. If you do, I know a cook's best friends. They're called "Fido" and "Hefty bags."

(One final heads-up: Remember that all ovens vary. You need to experiment with your own to figure it out.) Now let's go!

CHAPTER TWO

Rise and Shine— It's Breakfast Time

How much do I love breakfast? Beyond! I just don't relate to people who say, "I'm never hungry in the morning." What the heck is that about? Oh well, it's your loss. Personally, I can't wait to have breakfast every single day. It wakes me up and keeps me going, and I feel much better throughout the day knowing that I started out with a nice balanced meal.

The first recipe in this book is a tribute to my mom. She didn't cook a whole lot, but what she did make was always delicious. What follows is her famous Egg in the Hole, which was passed down from her mom, my beloved Grandma Mae. I'm so happy to start the recipes in this book with something traditional. Here's to you, Mom. And by the way, I love you.

My Mom's Egg in the Hole:
THE SINFUL
(Shown on right)

What little kid doesn't want to sleep in all day, even as their parents are trying to toss them out of bed and point them toward school? I thought of every reason in the book not to get my butt out of bed when I was little. Don't get me wrong. I enjoyed school after I got there. But getting me up in the morning was a nightmare of epic proportions.

It would start with Mom saying, "It's 6:30—time to get up!"

In the groggiest voice, I'd moan, "Oh, just 15 more minutes. Please!"

Now picture that it's 15 minutes later. Repeat the above scenario. Now repeat it again.

At about 7:25, Mom would come back into my bedroom expecting me to be up, showered, dressed, and ready to run out to the bus.

Was she kidding? I was still under the covers.

It was maddening for her, but Mom had a secret weapons of sorts. The only thing—and I mean the <u>only</u> thing—that made me get up early to go to school and avoid the waking-up drama was the heavenly smell that came from the kitchen when she made her famous Egg in the Hole.

The sourdough or egg bread sizzling in a mound of butter, with a perfect egg dropped into the center of the bread (where she'd made a hole from the garlic-salt cap), practically had me running into the kitchen with my homework in hand. I'd even sit at the table and wait for my plate to arrive. I looked like a baby bird with its mouth wide open.

Thank God Mom made this dish a few days a week for my sister, Wendy, and me, because I probably wouldn't have made it to school otherwise. Thanks, Mom!

Stuff You Need:

1 piece of white bread (I like sourdough)

2 tsp. butter or margarine

1 large egg

Salt and pepper (optional)

Hit It:

Take the cap off a seasoning jar (such as garlic salt). Put a piece of bread on a clean surface; place the cap in the center, press down firmly, and twist slightly, until you touch the surface below. Push the bread through the imprint and save the little circle of bread. You should have a perfect, and quite cute, hole in the bread.

Heat 1 tsp. butter in a skillet over medium heat—when it begins to sizzle, place the bread in the pan. Let it cook for 30 seconds or so, and then gently crack the egg into the hole so that the yolk doesn't break. (**Tip:** It's okay if the egg white runs down either side of the bread.) Throw in the little reserved circle of bread for an extra crispy bite!

Cook for approximately 1 minute; now lift the bread up with a spatula and peek at the underside—it should be nice and golden brown, and you should be dying to eat it by now. (Don't worry, that's totally normal.) Lift the bread and egg out of the pan with a wide spatula, and put the other teaspoon of butter in the pan. (**Tip:** Do this with your other hand and be careful not to burn yourself.) It should sizzle right away.

Flip the bread over, and let the egg cook to your desired consistency: You might like it runny so that you can mop up the yolk with the bread, or you might be like me—I like the yolk halfway cooked with a slight bit of runniness. Finish with a touch of salt and pepper if you like a little spice.

Serves 1 (how cute!).

Now Serving:

Enjoy with a tablespoon of ketchup. I also like to sprinkle on some onion powder when cooking this dish for an extra little kick.

My Mom's Egg in the Hole:
THE SKINNY

Cut a smaller slice of the bread and create a slightly bigger hole in the center. Don't eat the middle piece; instead, throw it away or feed it to the dog.

Spray a frying pan with Pam or a similar low-cal cooking spray, pour Egg Beaters in the center of the bread, and flip after about a minute on each side. Season well with salt, pepper, and a dash of onion powder.

Now you're ready to face the United Nations—or at least those snippy girls who drive you nuts at the office as they drone on and on about their low-cal dishes. In other words, you've just had an amazing breakfast without ruining your diet.

You Say Potato, I Say Frittata

I'm a huge fan of Ina Garten (aka the Barefoot Contessa from the Food Network, and author of many wonderful cookbooks). She's not only adorable, but her recipes are amazing. Do they turn out? Always. Do I respect her? To infinity. Do I trust her? From the moment I plop the first ingredients for her dishes into my shopping cart at the local market. Anyway, this is inspired by Ina—with a little kick of cayenne. Sometimes you need a little help waking up in the morning.

Stuff You Need:

8 Tbsp. unsalted butter (1 stick)

2 cups boiling potatoes, cut into ½" chunks (about 4 potatoes)

8 extra-large eggs

15 oz. ricotta cheese

12 oz. Gruyère cheese, grated
   (**Tip:** Just do it—it's so yummy.)

½ tsp. kosher salt

½ tsp. black pepper

⅛ tsp. garlic powder

⅛ tsp. onion powder

¾ cup fresh basil leaves, chopped

½ tsp. fresh or dried chives

⅛ tsp. cayenne pepper for zip (optional)

⅓ cup flour

¾ tsp. baking powder

Hit It:

Preheat oven to 350°. Melt 3 Tbsp. of butter in a 10" oven-proof omelette pan over medium-low heat. Add in the potatoes, turning them until they're cooked through; stir often for about 10 to 15 minutes.

Melt the remaining 5 Tbsp. of butter in a small dish in the microwave. Meanwhile, in a large bowl, whisk the eggs. Stir in the ricotta and Gruyère cheese; the melted butter; and the salt, pepper, garlic powder, onion powder, cayenne, basil, and chives. Sprinkle the flour and baking powder over the egg mixture, and stir in. Pour the egg mixture over the potatoes, and place the pan on the center rack of the oven.

Bake until it's browned and puffy (it's okay if it's a little softer in the middle). We're talking about 50 minutes to 1 hour here, which gives you plenty of time to get dressed and put on your makeup.

It's done when a knife inserted in the center comes out clean. Serve hot and moan!

Serves 6.

Now Serving:

This dish goes beautifully with some sliced strawberries and oranges.

Brunch Pie, Oh My!

This is a fantastic, fast brunch or supper dish that uses prepackaged seasonings, leftover chicken breasts, and muffin mix to save time.

Stuff You Need:

3 lbs. boneless, skinless chicken breasts, cut into 1" cubes

2 envelopes Lawry's Chicken Taco Spices & Seasonings Mix

Two 14-oz. cans of diced tomatoes and juice

3 cups (about 12 oz.) low-fat sharp cheddar cheese, grated (**Tip:** If you're feeling dangerous, substitute Sonoma low-fat pepper jack.)

1 can diced green chilis, undrained

1 **Fresh Corn-Muffin Crust** (see below)

Hit It:

Pre-heat oven to 350°. In a large mixing bowl, toss the chicken cubes in the taco seasoning. Add the tomatoes and juice, along with 1 cup of grated cheese. Spread the chicken-and-tomato mixture in a 13" x 9" baking dish, top with the chilis, and layer the remaining cheese over that. Prepare the muffin crust (below) and place it on top. Drop small spoonfuls of cheese evenly around the top of the pie, making sure that they're close together.

Bake for an hour, or until the crust is golden and the sauce is bubbling. Remove from the oven and let stand 15 minutes before serving.

Serves 6.

Fresh Corn-Muffin Crust

Stuff You Need:

One 8.5-oz. box corn-muffin mix (I like Jiffy brand)

1½ cups (about 12 oz.) fresh corn kernels scraped off the cob, or frozen sweet-corn kernels, thawed and drained

2 eggs

⅓ cup sour cream

Hit It:

In a medium mixing bowl, whisk the eggs with the sour cream. Combine the egg mixture with the muffin mix and corn, not mixing for more than 30 seconds or so. Batter will look lumpy.

You'll Always Remember Your First Quiche

Stuff You Need:

1 refrigerated ready-to-bake piecrust

4 eggs

2 cups whipping cream

1 tsp. sea or kosher salt

⅛ tsp. mace

⅛ tsp. pepper

6 oz. shredded Swiss or Gruyère cheese

1 Tbsp. Dijon mustard

⅓ cup cooked bacon, crumbled

⅓ cup mushrooms, sliced thinly, sautéed in butter, and allowed to release their juices (**Tip:** Reserve the juices for another use.)

Hit It:

Sauté the mushrooms and remove from butter; pat dry with a paper towel. Bring the piecrust to room temperature and line a 10"-deep pie plate with it (trim the edges if necessary). Using your fingertips, spread the Dijon mustard evenly around the inside of the crust.

In a large mixing bowl, beat the eggs with a fork and mix in the cream, salt, mace, and pepper. Preheat oven to 425°. Sprinkle bacon evenly around the piecrust, mound the shredded cheese in the center of it, and sprinkle mushrooms over the cheese. Pour the egg mixture over all, and carefully place into the preheated oven.

Bake for 15 minutes, then reduce the heat to 320°; continue baking for an additional 35 minutes or until the center of the quiche doesn't move when shaken and a toothpick inserted into the center comes out clean.

Serves 6.

It's "Worth" a Try Toast

This dish is indirectly inspired by my sister. When we were little, we used to love peanut butter on toast. Wendy would spread honey on hers, but I wasn't that crazy about honey as a child. (Actually, I don't even love it that much now.) But it's not like I was on a sugar strike—come on! I did love Mrs. Butterworth's syrup, though, so one day I decided to try it on my peanut-butter toast instead of honey. Wen thought I was nuts, but oh my God! I thought it was a knockout.

This is an easy breakfast if you're on the go; plus, you even get a little protein in there. These days, I use some pure maple syrup. Lord knows I'd be ill if I ate Mrs. Butterworth's, which is infinitely sweeter. Don't worry—this is still very rich and something that you shouldn't eat every single day. In a perfect world, I could eat it all the time . . . well, I dare to dream.

Stuff You Need:

1 slice of sourdough or challah bread

1 tsp. butter

2 Tbsp. Skippy or your favorite peanut butter (smooth or chunky)

⅛ to ¼ cup heated Mrs. Butterworth's or pure maple syrup

Hit It:

Toast the bread; heat the syrup in the microwave for 30 seconds or until hot (don't burn yourself!). When the toast is ready, place it on a plate, and spread butter and then peanut butter on it. Now pour the heated syrup all over it, and enjoy, enjoy, enjoy! How could anything be so darn good?!

Serves 1.

Egging You on Omelettes

I love eggs. If I have them in the morning, they leave me satisfied for the longest time. The funny thing is that I also wind up making better choices for lunch and dinner if I start my day with eggs. I can even do a no-carb breakfast, although my natural instinct is to have my eggs with a piece of toast or wrapped in a flour tortilla with melted cheese. For a rare treat, I'll even do a half a bagel with the eggs on it.

I'm always experimenting with omelettes, but there are a few I keep going back to because they taste really good. The following dishes are for one person. I usually eat breakfast before my husband is up, so I'm cooking for me, myself, and I—except if the dogs find my plate when I run for a quick phone call. (Willie, Olive, and Sammy, you're busted now!)

I use olive oil to cook my eggs in because it gives them a unique taste, plus it's a cleaner way to make them. But you can use butter, margarine, or Pam to cook yours—I'm not going to be eggs-acting here. (Sorry, I had to do one bad egg pun.)

Chive-Talking Eggs

Stuff You Need:

2 large eggs, whipped with 1 Tbsp.
    half-and-half, milk, or water
    with a wire whisk

1 tsp. fresh chives, minced

¼ cup mozzarella cheese and/or
    1 Tbsp. cream cheese

1 tsp. olive oil

A dash of onion powder

Salt and pepper to taste

Hit It:

Heat the olive oil in a medium nonstick skillet. Add the eggs and reduce the heat to low. Keep stirring and then add the cheese, onion powder, salt, and pepper. Stir around so the eggs don't burn. Just before the eggs are done, add the chives.

CHIVE-TALKING EGGS

(Egging You on Omelettes, cont'd.)

Where the Buffalo Cheese Roams Eggs

Stuff You Need:

2 large eggs, beaten

3 slices fresh buffalo mozzarella cheese

⅛ cup chopped tomatoes

1 Tbsp. fresh basil leaves, chopped

Salt and pepper to taste

1 tsp. olive oil

Hit It:

Heat the olive oil in a medium-size nonstick skillet. Add eggs and turn the heat to low. Stir the eggs; add the cheese, basil, and tomatoes; and salt and pepper to taste. Cook until the eggs are done.

Peppy Eggs

Stuff You Need:

2 large eggs, beaten in a small bowl

6 slices turkey pepperoni
   (**Tip:** I like the thin kind made by Hormel.)

¼ cup broccoli florets

¼ cup shredded mozzarella

1 tsp. olive oil

A dash of onion powder

A dash of garlic powder

A dash of cayenne pepper

Salt and pepper to taste

Hit It:

Heat the olive oil in a medium-size nonstick skillet. Add the broccoli and cook for 1 minute, then add the pepperoni and cook for 1 minute more. Add the eggs, and turn the heat to low. Stir the eggs, sprinkle with onion powder, garlic powder, and cayenne pepper; salt and pepper to taste. Add the cheese, and stir so that the eggs don't stick.

---

911 Moment!

It's pretty easy to screw up eggs, since you can easily overcook them. They need to be prepared in a pan heated on a high flame—then you should put in the eggs and immediately turn the heat down to a low flame, otherwise they'll get browned and burned. Once they get that way, there's no going back.

You're Stacked
(Easy-Style Pancakes with Fillings)

There's nothing yummier in the morning than that first bite of pancakes dripping with some special syrup. Close your eyes for a sec and just imagine it . . . okay, now wake up. Really, wake up!

This recipe can be done with either homemade batter or with your favorite mix. What's gene is the fillings. I love to make pancakes this way because I always want more flavor and, well, more of everything—and give it to me twice yesterday.

Stuff You Need:

1¼ cups flour

2 tsp. baking powder

1 Tbsp. sugar

1 Tbsp. brown sugar

¾ tsp. salt

1⅓ cups milk

1 egg, slightly beaten

3 Tbsp. vegetable oil

Butter or Crisco for cooking
   (Crisco is better, as it won't burn like butter)

Hot maple syrup

Hit It:

In a large mixing bowl, mix the flour, sugars, baking powder, and salt. Add the milk, egg, and vegetable oil. Stir until blended, but not completely smooth (there should be a few lumps).

Heat a few tablespoons of butter or Crisco on a griddle or in a skillet until hot, but not burning or smoking. Pour pancakes measuring about ¼ cup on top of the griddle. Make a few at a time, adding butter if necessary to keep things stick free. Cook until the bubbles on top of the pancakes start bursting. Turn over with a spatula when undersides are golden.

Serve with a little powdered sugar sprinkled on top, along with a sprig of mint for that added touch.

Makes 12–15 pancakes.

Now for the Really Good Stuff:

Follow the directions above, or you may substitute your favorite prepackaged mix. After pouring the batter into the pan, drop 10 or so chocolate chips and a few banana slices into them. Turn the pancakes over and continue to cook. (**Tip:** It might be a little messy, but so what? It tastes divine!)

Variations:

- Peanut-butter chips and bananas. Yowza!

- One step further into calorie-land is chocolate chips *and* peanut-butter chips. Mind blowing!

- How about blueberries and peach slices? Make sure that the peach slices are fresh, peeled, patted dry, and sliced in a way that's not too thick, but not paper thin either. Heaven!

- Finally, for you savory-loving types, mix into the batter (before cooking) 1 cup corn kernels and ½ cup cooked crumbled bacon.

BAKED APPLE PANCAKES

Send in the Clouds
(Baked-Apple Pancakes)

Lovely and heavenly!

Stuff You Need:

½ cup butter

5 Fuji apples

6 eggs

1½ cups flour

1½ cups milk

1½ tsp. vanilla

¼ tsp. salt

6 Tbsp. plus 1 tsp. sugar, separated

1 tsp. cinnamon

3 Tbsp. light brown sugar

Hit It:

Melt the butter in a 13″ x 9″ Pyrex dish in a 400° oven. Peel, core, and slice the apples; evenly distribute the slices in the pan with the hot melted butter and return it to the oven.

In a large mixing bowl, combine the eggs, flour, milk, vanilla, salt, and 6 Tbsp. of sugar until blended. In a small dish, mix together the cinnamon, brown sugar, and 1 tsp. sugar; set aside for a moment. Remove the pan with the apples from the oven, and quickly pour the batter over them. (**Tip:** Do not mix!) Dust the top with the cinnamon mixture.

Bake for 20 to 30 minutes, or until puffy and golden brown.

Serves 6.

Love Muffins

Stuff You Need:

1½ cups all-purpose flour

¼ cup sugar

¼ cup light brown sugar

1½ tsp. baking powder

¼ tsp. baking soda

¼ tsp. salt

½ cup (1 stick) unsalted butter

1 cup sour cream

1 large egg

1½ tsp. vanilla

¾ cup semisweet chocolate chips

¾ cup toasted pecans

Hit It:

Preheat oven to 400° and line 12 (⅓ cup) muffin cups with paper liners, or use a silicone muffin pan. Lightly mix together the flour, sugar, baking powder, baking soda, and salt in a large mixing bowl, lifting and fluffing these ingredients together with a fork. Melt the butter; in a small bowl, whisk it together with the sour cream, egg, and vanilla. Stir the butter mixture, chocolate chips, and nuts into the flour mixture until just combined.

Divide the batter among muffin cups, filling them ⅔ of the way, and bake on the middle rack of the oven until golden and a tester comes out clean, about 20 minutes.

Makes a dozen muffins.

Now Serving:

Serve with fresh fruit . . . and a nice strong cup of coffee!

Good Morning French Toast:
THE SINFUL

Ooh la la! That's how I feel about French toast as a way to start the day . . . especially when it's topped with some fresh seasonal berries and served with some orange juice or coffee. Please! You could serve me this breakfast in a Dumpster and I'd still be happy. (Thanks to Ina Garten of The Food Network for the inspiration.)

Stuff You Need:

1 loaf challah bread, sliced into ¾" slices (**Huh?** Challah is a Jewish egg bread that's such a delight I call it the best bread on the planet. Ask for it at your supermarket or bakery.)

6 large eggs

1 Tbsp. unsalted butter

1 tsp. vegetable oil

1 cup milk

½ cup heavy cream

1 tsp. honey

1 tsp. sugar

½ tsp. vanilla extract (**Tip:** It's worth it to invest in a good-quality, gourmet-type pure vanilla extract.)

1 tsp. grated orange zest (which I happen to think is the secret ingredient)

Hit It:

In a large shallow bowl, whisk the eggs, cream, milk, honey, sugar, vanilla, and orange zest. Soak as many slices of the challah as you can fit into the bowl with the egg mixture for 5 minutes (carefully turn each slice over one time).

Heat up a mixture of the butter and vegetable oil in a huge skillet over medium heat. Add the already-soaked slices to the pan, and cook for about 2 to 3 minutes on each side or until they have a nice golden color to them. Repeat with the remaining bread slices, adding more butter and oil as you need. (**Tip:** If you want to keep the first few slices warm after they come out of the pan, preheat the oven to 250° and place them in a dish. Remember to cover with foil so that they don't burn.)

Serves 8.

Now Serving:

Sprinkle these "sacred toasts" with powdered sugar and serve with warm, real maple syrup. Mmm, good!

Good Morning French Toast:
THE SKINNY

Try the original recipe with low-cal bread, skim milk, and no-cal cooking spray or I Can't Believe It's Not Butter. Add half of a cut apple sprinkled with cinnamon and Splenda to the pan, and cook until slightly brown. Serve everything with sugar-free or low-cal syrup. (You can also heat up sugar-free applesauce in the microwave and use it as a syrup or a topping.)

Every Day's a Hollandaise
(Grandma Betty's Fancy Eggs Benedict)

My mom's husband, Daniel, has a mom who's a fabulous cook. She lives in Canada and is always sharing her treasured recipes. In fact, when I asked her for one of her best dishes, she said, "I have tons—where do I start? How long is this book?" Thanks, Grandma Betty, and I'll do a few extra miles on my treadmill to work this one off. It's worth it.

Stuff You Need:

4 croissants, halved lengthwise

1 pkg. Knorr hollandaise sauce

2 Tbsp. fresh lemon juice

8 eggs

3 Tbsp. water

¼ tsp. dried parsley flakes

A small pinch cayenne pepper

2 Tbsp. butter, divided

Salt and pepper to taste

4 slices precooked ham

1 avocado, sliced (optional)

Hit It:

Preheat oven to 150°. Put the croissants on 4 (oven-suitable) plates and place in the oven. We're heating these puppies up! Prepare the hollandaise sauce according to the package; add the lemon juice and set aside, covered with foil, until ready to use.

In a large mixing bowl, add the eggs and water, whipping with a wire whisk or a fork until combined and lighter in color; add the parsley and cayenne pepper. In a nonstick skillet, melt 1 Tbsp. of the butter over medium heat; add the eggs and turn the flame down to low. Add salt and pepper to taste, and stir the eggs until they're cooked. Put the eggs aside and cover with foil.

Add the cooked ham to the skillet and heat for a minute or until hot. Now take the croissants out of the oven and put ¼ Tbsp. of the butter on each bottom half, followed by one slice of ham and ¼ portion of the eggs. Cover with the top half of the croissant and then put each one onto the heated plates from the oven. Pour some hollandaise sauce over the croissants and garnish with avocado slices. What a way to wake up!

Serves 4.

Aloha Granola

Excuse me for a minute while I'm crunching away, but I have to tell you a little something about breakfast cereal: You can make the best kind right in your own kitchen! It's much easier than you think, but I suggest that you keep the leftovers in the freezer because they're that good. (Thanks to Ina Garten of The Food Network for the inspiration.)

Stuff You Need:

4½ cups old-fashioned rolled oats

½ cup roasted macadamia nuts,
  roughly chopped

½ cup roasted, unsalted cashews,
  roughly chopped

2 cups sliced almonds

2 cups sweetened coconut, shredded *(mmm)*

¾ cup vegetable oil

1 cup honey

¼ cup dried pineapple chunks

½ cup dried mango, chopped

⅛ cup banana chips (sweet, not salty)

1 cup dried strawberries

1 cup dried cranberries

Hit It:

Preheat the oven to 350°. (Don't eat all the dried fruit before you make the dish! I can see you!)

In a large bowl, toss to combine the oats, coconut, and almonds. Whisk together the oil and honey in a separate small bowl and pour over the oat mixture. Stir with a big wooden spoon until all the nuts and oats are well coated, and pour the mixture onto a 13" x 18" baking sheet.

Bake, stirring occasionally with a spatula until it turns a nice golden-brown color. This should take about 45 minutes, depending on your own preferences. When your cereal is done, remove it from the oven and let it cool, stirring occasionally. Add all the delicious dried fruit and remaining nuts, toss, and get ready for your loved ones to dive in. Stop for a second and look at this dish—it's cool to be proud.

Store the leftovers in airtight containers and try to control yourself.

Makes approximately 4 cups.

Q: A "special guest" has slept over for the first time. What do you do?

A: **Here are two distinct menu plans for this very dilemma:**

1. "The Sun Is Shining, the Birds Are Chirping, and the World Is a Beautiful Place" Breakfast

Sneak out of bed early and whip up the following first meal that will warm his or her stomach.

Menu:
Egging You on Omelette (page12)
Love Muffins (page 17)
Hickory smoked bacon served crispy
Freshly squeezed orange juice

Now Serving:
Try to find Peet's coffee (or any other gourmet brand with some vanilla in it). I also love vanilla-nut and vanilla-and-caramel creamers.

Carnie Aside-a:
Place a fresh daisy on the tray.

Bottom Line:
You'll have one satisfied guest—in fact, he or she may *never* leave!

2. "The Mourning After" Meal

This is otherwise known as the "Please, Dear God, Make This Person Leave" Last Meal.

Menu:
Watery eggs, undercooked and oversalted
Yesterday's coffee,s served cold
Milk that smells funky
A dead or plastic flower

Carnie's Hints:

- Complain while cooking and make loud, crashing noises in the kitchen.

- Make the kitchen a mess.

- Spill the dish while you serve it to him or her.

- Let your dog beg next to your guest and drool on their feet. Don't be surprised if he or she winds up giving the "food" to your furry friend. Remember that your dog will eat anything . . . and fast! This fact moves things along.

- Place his or her car keys near the food, signaling that your guest needs to leave ASAP. If that doesn't work, offer to warm up the car while he or she eats. It doesn't matter if it's 80° and sunny outside.

Bottom Line:
You won't be getting any phone calls for future stays. You won't be getting any calls, period.

A Perfect Parfait

This is a great breakfast, but it's also a great low-cal dessert that looks really beautiful in a parfait or sundae dish.

Stuff You Need:

½ cup mixed sliced fruit, such as strawberries, raspberries, blackberries, blueberries, peaches, or plums

½ cup vanilla, lemon, or strawberry yogurt (or use your favorite flavor)

½ cup granola (you can use the store-bought kind or my **Aloha Granola** on page 20)

1 tsp. milk chocolate shavings (**Tip**: Try to quickly put the rest of the chocolate away, because it's so tempting if it's just sitting there. This is also an optional ingredient.)

½ cup frozen whipped topping or freshly whipped cream (divide into two ¼ cups)

1 spring of fresh mint leaves

Hit It:

In a small bowl, mix ¼ cup of the whipped topping with 1 cup yogurt. Place the following—in this order—in a parfait glass, sundae glass, or dessert bowl:

- 💜 ½ of the fruit
- 💜 A thick layer of granola
- 💜 The other ½ of the fruit
- 💜 A dollop of whipped topping
- 💜 Some mint leaves for garnish (and the chocolate shavings, if you wish)

Serves 1–2.

CHAPTER THREE

Let's Muncha on Luncha

If you're a size zero, baby, and you haven't had lunch since 1978 . . . well, you have my blessing. Have a wonderful life.

But I don't quite get it.

I have to eat breakfast, lunch, *and* dinner because it's too awful to think of missing even one of these meals. Now I know what you're thinking: *Carnie, I love lunch, but I don't have time to do much more than drive through an establishment with some yellow arches.* Trust me when I say that there are ways to make yourself fabulous lunches that take almost no time in the kitchen. You can even make them in advance for the workweek. So please don't forget your midday love festival. You deserve it.

And no offense to the old "turkey, mayo, and cheese on white bread," but you can do much better.

I Can Name That Tuna . . . Salad

Let me just say for the record that I adore tuna. When I was pregnant, it was pure torture to only be able to have six ounces every two weeks. I practically cried—for me, this was worse than morning sickness! There's mercury in tuna, so you've gotta be careful, even if you're not preggers. But I just adore it, whether it's raw, cooked, or in a salad. Yummy!

Basic Tuna Salad

Stuff You Need:

1½ cups of canned tuna (two 6-oz. cans of white albacore in water), well drained

½ cup finely chopped celery

½ cup mayonnaise (**Tip:** If you want to go Skinny, do light or fat-free mayo or ⅔ plain yogurt and ⅓ regular mayo. By the way, a certain whip is no miracle for me. Don't even bother!)

3 Tbsp. lemon juice

1 tsp. minced parsley for garnish

Hit It:

Mix everything well—it's that easy. Serves 4.

Sometimes You Feel Like a Nut Tuna Salad

Stuff You Need:

18-oz. white albacore in water (this means one 12-oz. can and one 6-oz. can), well drained

¼ cup celery, finely chopped

⅛ cup sweet pickle relish

1 Tbsp. minced red onion

1 Tbsp. relish juice

1 Tbsp. lemon juice

½ cup mayo

¼ cup chopped cashews (**Tip:** Take a knife and roughly chop them, but be careful not to get them all over the kitchen. And don't eat the rest of the can of cashews! This recipe already has mayo in it, and you don't need the extra calories.)

8 red grapes, cut in half the long way

A dash of kosher salt and pepper

1 tsp. finely minced fresh parsley

Hit It:

Flake the tuna well so that there aren't any lumps. Combine all ingredients well, gently folding in the grapes at the end. Prepare yourself for tuna with a little kick!

Serves 4–6.

Now Serving:

I love to put this in lettuce cups or over a salad (which makes it Skinny!), or I'll make half a sandwich out of it. I adore Seven Seas Red Wine Vinaigrette over the salad. Delish!

Variation and Additions
Add the following to the Basic Tuna Salad:

💜 **Curry Me Away**
   1–2 tsp. curry powder and a pinch of sugar

💜 **An Apple a Day**
   1 cup unpeeled Fuji or red apples, diced
   ½ cup walnuts, chopped

💜 **A Dilly of a Recipe**
   1 Tbsp. dill relish
   1 Tbsp. chives

Now Serving:

This is fun! You can stuff any of these tuna recipes into a seeded tomato and top with your favorite cheese. Pop under the broiler or in a toaster oven until the cheese melts. (P.S. Cut the top off a tomato like you're removing its hat by cutting ½" below the stem. Watch the tomato carefully in the broiler because it can become the towering inferno of flaming veggies quickly. We're not looking for a bonfire here!)

For the Skinny, stuff into lettuce cups or a tomato (sans cheese). And, obviously, you can make a sandwich with it. I love tuna salad on baguettes or ciabatta bread.

---

911 Moment!

You put in too much mayo and think that your tuna is sunk. Don't despair—just add more tuna. In other words, be careful that you don't add too much mayo! (You could also give the overly mayo-ed tuna to the neighborhood supermodel. She could use the calories.)

Viva Las Veggies Mexican Salad:
THE SINFUL

You aren't spinning the roulette wheel here—this is a sure bet for a delicious lunch for yourself or some friends.

This is also a great recipe to make in advance because you don't need to thaw the frozen veggies. Added to the joy is the fact that the salad will be chilled when you're ready to serve it. ¡Olé!

Stuff You Need:

One 12-oz. bag frozen sweet-corn kernels

One 12-oz. bag frozen tiny, sweet green peas

One 14-oz. can of kidney beans, drained and rinsed

5 scallions, trimmed and sliced including 3" of green tops)

4 ribs of celery, sliced in half lengthwise, then into thin crescents

1 pint of tiny, sweet grape tomatoes or small cherry tomatoes, washed and stemmed if necessary

One 12-oz. brick of firm cheese diced into ½" cubes (cheddar, jack, or a combination of both works well)

1 small can of sliced black olives

1 large ripe avocado, peeled, pitted, and cut into 1" cubes, then lightly tossed with lemon juice (to prevent browning)

1 red and 1 green bell pepper, each stemmed, seeded, and diced into 1" pieces

⅛ cup of fresh cilantro, washed with stems removed, and finely chopped (reserve 1 Tbsp. for garnish)

1 Tbsp. fresh parsley, minced

1½ cups of roughly broken tortilla chips

Dressing:

½ cup mayonnaise

½ cup sour cream

½ cup mild salsa (I like the kind made by Pace)

2 Tbsp. catsup

Hit It:

Combine the dressing ingredients in a small bowl and mix well. In a large mixing bowl, combine the dressing and all the salad ingredients except the avocados, and toss. Gently fold in the avocados last so that they retain their shape. Top with the reserved chopped cilantro and let sit for at least 30 minutes before serving.

Serves 6 as a main dish or 10 as a side.

Carnie Aside-a:

Remember, you put in the ingredients frozen and let the salad sit out on the counter—allow it to thaw while you do other things. It's gene.

Viva Las Veggies Mexican Salad:
THE SKINNY

More fresh vegetables have been added here, along with low-fat dairy products and a sugar-free sweetener for the dressing. The starchier, heavier vegetables have been cut way back, and the fattier ingredients such as avocado, olives, and chips have been used with a much lighter hand and/or replaced with low-fat substitutes.

Stuff You Need:

One 10-oz. box frozen sweet-corn kernels

Half of a 10-oz. box frozen tiny, sweet green peas

Half of a 14-oz. can of kidney beans, drained and rinsed

5 scallions, trimmed and sliced (including 3" of green tops)

8 ribs of celery, sliced in half lengthwise, then into thin crescents

2 pints of tiny, sweet grape tomatoes or small cherry tomatoes, washed and stemmed if necessary

One 12-oz. brick of 2%-fat cheese diced into ½" cubes (cheddar, jack, or a combination of both works well)

1 Tbsp. sliced black olives for garnish

Half of a large ripe avocado, peeled, pitted, and cut into ½" cubes, then lightly tossed with lemon juice (to prevent browning)

2 red and 2 green bell peppers, each stemmed, seeded, and diced into 1" pieces

⅛ cup fresh cilantro, washed with stems removed, and finely chopped (reserve 1 Tbsp. for garnish)

1 Tbsp. fresh parsely, minced

1½ cups of roughly broken baked tortilla chips

Dressing:

½ cup light mayonnaise

½ cup nonfat sour cream

½ cup mild salsa (I like the kind made by Pace)

2 Tbsp. sugar-free catsup

1 packet Splenda

Hit It:

Combine the dressing ingredients in a small bowl and mix well. In a large mixing bowl, combine the dressing and all the salad ingredients except the avocados, olives, and half of the tortilla chips; toss to combine. Gently fold in the avocados last to retain their shape, and top with the reserved chopped cilantro, olives, and chips. Let sit for at least 30 minutes before serving. Watch your guests come back for seconds or thirds.

Serves 6 as a main course or 10 as a side.

Get Your Greens Spinach Salad

This recipe is a great way to get your greens in for the day, plus this bowl of "the good stuff" is filled with iron. So healthy, so tasty. I like this salad paired with the raspberry dressing below, but you could easily do a nice red-wine vinaigrette or your favorite Italian. I also like to serve it with something warm and hearty, like the butternut-squash soup on page 50 or the corn-tomato bisque on page 45.

Stuff You Need:

1 bag prewashed baby-spinach leaves

½ of a Bermuda onion (red onion), cut through the middle and then sliced into ringlets

1 cup large white button mushrooms, sliced (this is optional—omit it if you hate fungus)

8–10 slices bacon, cooked and crumbled (**Tip:** Don't overcook your bacon, or it will become bitter.)

1 ripe Anjou pear, thinly sliced lengthwise and patted with lemon juice to avoid discoloration (**Tip:** No canned pears. Ick. If pears aren't in season, you can substitute one navel orange, separated into sections with membrane and seeds removed.)

One 6-oz. block of good quality feta or blue cheese, drained and crumbled roughly

¾ cup praline pecans or walnuts (**Hint:** Wear a muzzle so you don't eat all the candied pecans before they hit the salad . . . we've all been there.)

Hit It:

In a large mixing bowl, combine the first 5 ingredients and mix well. Top with feta or blue cheese and pecans (if you like), along with the salad dressing of your choice.

Serves 2 as a main dish or 4–6 as a side dish.

Raspberry Dressing

Stuff You Need:

½ cup extra-virgin olive oil

¼ cup raspberry vinegar

⅛ cup orange juice

½ of a clove of garlic, finely minced (or ½ tsp garlic paste)

1 Tbsp. raspberry jam

1 Tbsp. Dijon mustard

Salt and pepper to taste

Hit It:

Whisk the Dijon mustard and raspberry jam together in a small bowl. Add the orange juice in, a few drops at a time, so there are no lumps; add garlic and mix well. Slowly stir the raspberry vinegar into the mustard mixture, making sure that it's "making friends" with everything else. Drizzle the olive oil into this mixture very slowly, while constantly whisking until emulsified. Add salt and pepper to taste. Dip your finger in and check it out. Mmm . . . it's special.

Dresses 1 large salad.

My Own Chinese Chix Salad
(with Too-Pooped-to-Poppy Seed Dressing)

I think this rivals anything you'll find in a good restaurant—the dressing especially is a showstopper. The best part is that you just toss all the ingredients and shake 'em up (I add lots of mandarin oranges because they're my husband's favorite). Trust me: It's soooo easy!

Stuff You Need:

½ head of iceberg lettuce and
    ½ of a head of romaine,
    cleaned, dried, and chopped

1½ cups Swiss cheese, shredded

1 cup salted and toasted cashews

3 chicken breasts, cooked and shredded

One 10-oz. can mandarin oranges

2–3 Tbsps. green onion, chopped

1 cup croutons (I like the ones with sea
    salt and olive oil)

Dressing:

1 cup vegetable oil

⅓ cup white vinegar

¾ cup sugar

1 tsp. French's yellow mustard

½ tsp. onion, grated

½ Tbsp. poppy seeds

Salt to taste

Hit It:

Make the dressing first! Whisk all ingredients in a bowl until thick and combined. In a medium bowl, toss the shredded chicken breast with 3 Tbsp. of the dressing and a pinch of salt and pepper. Give it a rest in the refrigerator.

When you're ready to eat, toss the lettuce, cheese, cashews, chicken, and onion together in a large bowl. Pour the amount of dressing you'd like onto the salad and toss well. Garnish with mandarin oranges and croutons. Enjoy!

Serves 4–6 as a main dish, or 8 as a side dish.

Turn the Beet Around Salad
(with Walnut-Tarragon Dressing)

Let's be honest: Not everyone loves beets, but they're healthy, and I adore them. This is a beautiful and colorful salad that's a nice alternative to your everyday greens. Serve it with a sprinkle of the amazing walnut-tarragon dressing that follows.

Stuff You Need:

Two 14-oz. cans shoestring beets, drained (they should be the julienne type)

One 6-oz. (approximately) package blue or feta cheese

¾ cup toasted walnuts

⅛–¼ cup diced or thinly sliced red onions

Butter lettuce leaves for serving

Dressing:

½ cup walnut oil

⅛ cup tarragon vinegar (or ⅛ cup white-wine vinegar and 1 tsp. minced tarragon)

½ tsp. grainy mustard

Salt and pepper to taste

Hit It:

In a small bowl, whisk the vinegar and mustard together. Slowly drizzle in the oil while continuing to whisk until the dressing is emulsified. Salt and pepper to taste.

In a medium-size bowl, toss the red onions and beets lightly with the dressing. (**Tip:** Hey, be careful not to break up your beets. They're fragile.) Set aside if serving immediately, or place in the fridge if you're preparing in advance. Just before serving, fold in the walnuts and sprinkle with feta or blue cheese. You're done! Don't you love quickies like this one? I do!

Serves 4, or 8–10 as an appetizer. But remember, it's very rich.

My Big Fat Greek Pasta Salad

This recipe is in honor of actress Nia Vardalos, who wrote and starred in one of my favorite movies, My Big Fat Greek Wedding. It was an unbeatable performance, and I hope that this pasta salad lives up to the film! This a wonderful summer (or anytime) dish that's light and satisfying. I love feta cheese on anything, and this is an excuse to eat it with abandon. It's also great to bring to a potluck or barbecue.

Stuff You Need:

One 16-oz. box of fusilli or rotini pasta, cooked according to the box, but slightly al dente (**Huh?** *Al dente* means cooked, but not mushy—in other words, it's still a little bit chewy)

1 Tbsp. extra-virgin olive oil

1 pint small, sweet grape tomatoes, washed and stemmed if necessary

1 hothouse cucumber, thinly sliced into rounds

½ of a red onion, quartered and thickly sliced into strips

1 red and 1 green bell pepper, stemmed, seeded, and cut into 2" strips

2 Tbsp. capers

1 cup kalamata olives, pitted

1 block (8 oz.) sheep's-milk feta cheese, cut into chunks

½ tsp. dried oregano

Dressing:

⅔ cup extra-virgin olive oil

¼ cup fresh lemon juice

1 clove garlic, shaved lengthwise into paper-thin slices (**Tip:** This is easier than it sounds. You have to do it really carefully with a very sharp knife. Put on an oven mitt when you do so that you keep all your fingers and avoid the smell. To get the odor of garlic or onion off your hands, rub them on stainless steel, like a measuring cup, under cold running water. It's amazing—it really works!)

2 Tbsp. white vinegar

1 tsp. honey

2 tsp. finely chopped fresh oregano

1 tsp. grainy mustard

½ tsp. salt and ¼ tsp. fresh ground black pepper

(**Tip:** If you don't want to make the dressing from scratch, then use one jar of Athens Feta Cheese Dressing with Herbs and toss well. If you do so, add an extra pinch of salt to taste.)

Hit It:

Cook and drain the pasta, and gently toss with 1 Tbsp. olive oil and oregano. Allow to completely cool. In a small bowl, whisk together the lemon juice, vinegar, honey, garlic, oregano, mustard, salt, and pepper. Slowly whisk in the olive oil until it emulsifies. Chill in the refrigerator until needed. (**Tip:** If you don't have time to make the dressing, you can use ½ cup feta cheese marinated in olive oil and herbs. They also have great Greek dressings at most supermarkets.)

Place the tomatoes, cucumber, onion, and bell peppers in a large bowl; gently fold in the cooled pasta. Remove the dressing from the fridge, whisk again, and drizzle over the pasta and vegetables, tossing well to distribute evenly and to make sure that some of each of the ingredients is displayed in an attractive way. Cut the feta into rough 1½" chunks and sprinkle over the salad; add the olives and capers and toss well. Remember that a lot of the little pieces will fall to the bottom—don't forget to dig them up when you serve this dish. Garnish with a few additional pieces of feta and olives and serve.

Serves 8.

The Skinny:

Use only 1 cup pasta, and reduce the dressing by half.

I'm a Greek Goddess
Salad Dressing

Obviously this is great on salads, but every now and then I like to dunk cooked-chicken cutlets or skewers into this dressing. It's a fantastic dip, and it takes the "boring" out of chicken. Sure, the dressing gives it a little taste of fat, but you're not getting too much.

Stuff You Need:

2 cups mayonnaise

1¼ cups sour cream

½ cup fresh parsley, minced

⅓ cup capers, minced

¼ cup green onions, chopped
  (include the white part)

1 tsp. fresh tarragon, minced

2 Tbsp. tarragon vinegar

2 Tbsp. fresh lemon juice

2 anchovy fillets, minced

1 Tbsp. anchovy paste

1 clove garlic (**Tip:** Place in a garlic press or
  smash by using the back of a knife, crushing
  garlic into a paste.)

Hit It:
  Just mix it all up!
  Yields 1 quart.

Ana's Greek Salad Dressing

Let's take a minute to talk about Ana Scandalis, my dear friend Vasili's mom, and her Greek cooking. She's so amazing. For example, she likes to take an entire white onion, peel it, and cut it into thin slices. Next, she places the onion slices in a bowl covered with kosher salt and water. Then she squeezes the onions, salt, and water until the onions become translucent. She gets all the salt off the onions by continually rinsing them with cold water. The onions take on a sweet flavor and remove that pungent aftertaste you get when you eat them raw. Yum! I also really love this recipe for her salad dressing. Thanks, Ana. ♥

Stuff You Need:

½ cup red-wine vinegar

1 tsp. salt

¼ tsp. freshly ground black pepper

1½ tsp. dried oregano

½ tsp. dried tarragon

1 Tbsp. fresh lemon juice

1 cup safflower oil

½ cup extra-virgin olive oil

1 clove garlic (**Tip:** Place in a garlic press
  or smash by using the back of a knife,
  crushing garlic into a paste.)

Hit It:
  Combine the first 7 ingredients in a small bowl and let stand for 15 minutes. Add oil gradually and blend well. Adjust seasoning to taste
  Dresses 1 large salad or makes 2 cups.

**Garlic Method When Using
a Wooden Salad Bowl:**
  Cut the garlic clove in half and place the cut sides down on the inside of the bowl. Rub the entire bowl's surface with the garlic, then add your salad greens and the dressing.

Loco for Quesadillas

The other night I had a strange dream where there was only one food left to eat on Earth. But it wasn't so bad . . . I was wandering around fields of beautifully homemade quesadillas.

I probably have some kind of quesadilla every single day because I love tortillas, both flour and corn, but eating them out of the bag with no topping is just plain boring. (Unless there's a cute old Mexican woman making them in front of you and then brushing the hot tortillas with butter. I guess I could make this little exception.) But get out some ingredients like cheese and chicken, and now we're talkin'!

Here's what I love about quesadillas: They're easy and fast. They also look great when you cut them into wedges and serve them with cool garnishes such as sour cream, chopped tomatoes, black olives, fresh cilantro, and sliced avocados (or the guacamole on page 69). The bottom line is that quesadillas make me happy. I especially love when they're a little bit crunchy. If you're really impatient or in a hurry, the microwave will do, but the gene way to make them is by using a grill pan with a drop of olive oil. A plain old skillet does great, too.

We have to stop talking about this now. I'm getting hungry, and the skillet is out. . . .

Stuff You Need:

1 flour tortilla

Any of the fillings below:

- 💜 ¼–½ cup mozzarella, 1 Tbsp. grilled corn, 3 grilled shrimp (tails removed), and a sprinkle of goat cheese and chives

- 💜 ⅛ cup sautéed mushrooms; 1 tsp. green chilis; ¼–½ cup Jarlsberg, mozzarella, or jack cheese

- 💜 ¼–½ cup mozzarella, 3–4 slices zucchini, 1 Tbsp. corn, ⅛ cup broccoli florets, ⅛ cup sliced mushrooms, and ⅛ cup diced red peppers (this is my fave)

- 💜 ½ cup mozzarella or jack cheese, ¼ cup thinly sliced steak, ¼ cup sliced onions, ¼ cup each diced red and green peppers, a pinch of garlic powder, salt, chili powder, and/or fajita seasoning

- 💜 ¼ cup diced ham and ½ cup shredded pepper-jack cheese (this is best on corn tortillas)

Hit It:

If you're working with veggies, steam or sauté them first. Take a lightly greased pan, place it on medium heat, and throw the tortilla in it. Put the ingredients in on one side of the tortilla, then fold it over. Cook on both sides until cheese is melted or gets a golden color.

Serves 1.

Now Serving:

I like to start with a little green salad or some fresh fruit before my quesadilla. Yum!

911 Moment!

If you see smoke, it's time to turn the quesadilla over or take the thing out the pan. In other words, watch these babies carefully because they burn quickly.

Dreamy Creamy Baked-Tomato Crostini

This dish will impress because it's full of flavors and bright colors. And what's better than basil? It's God's gift. This is a very tasty lunch, especially when served with iced tea with fresh mint leaves.

Stuff You Need:

6 large ripe Roma tomatoes, seeded and cut in half lengthwise, stem ends trimmed

1½ cups heavy cream

½ cup crème fraîche

2 cloves garlic, crushed

1 small bunch basil, leaves and stalks separated

1 tsp. sugar

1 Tbsp. mixed herbs, chopped (parsley, tarragon, dill, and chervil are all nice choices)

4 slices of country-style bread, toasted and rubbed with garlic and olive oil

8 oz. buffalo mozzarella cheese

1 Tbsp. Parmesan cheese, grated

Fresh black pepper

Hit It:

Preheat the oven to 375°. Take an ovenproof dish (such as a flat, oval casserole), rub the inside lightly with olive oil, and place the tomatoes inside, cut sides up. Bake for 10 minutes.

Put the cream, crème fraîche, garlic, basil stalks, and sugar in a saucepan and simmer until reduced by ⅓. Give a rough chop to the basil leaves and then add to the mixture in the saucepan; pour mixture over the tomatoes and put the whole thing back in the oven for an additional 15 minutes. Note that the cream will thicken and "blush" from the tomatoes.

Sprinkle the chopped herbs on the toasted bread, and then slice the mozzarella into 6 slices. When the tomatoes are cooked, remove from the dish, place 3 halves on each piece of toast, sprinkle with Parmesan, and top with a slice of mozzarella. Place on a baking sheet and cook for an additional 5 minutes, or until cheese begins to melt. Take a whiff of the air around you . . . they should bottle that smell. Remove from the oven and place on a warm plate. Pour the reduced basil cream around the tomatoes, and top it all with some freshly ground black pepper.

Serves 2–4.

Burger Queen: Two Fab Patties

I love all my vegan friends—they're fabulous. With that said, I have to add this next sentence: I need my meat.

The following burgers are a great lunch if you're hungry, or they also make a good dinner. Serve them to some nonvegan friends and they'll give you the crown!

I'm Not Blue Burger

Stuff You Need:

1 lb. ground sirloin (7% fat)

½ cup blue cheese, crumbled

1 cup onion ringlets, grilled

¼ tsp. garlic powder

1 Tbsp. thyme, fresh or dried

¼ tsp. black pepper

½ tsp. salt

A pinch of ground cayenne pepper

8 slices cooked bacon (optional)

Hit It:

In a large mixing bowl, combine the beef, garlic powder, thyme, salt, pepper, and cayenne. Roll the mixture into 8 equal-sized balls, then flatten each between the palms of your hands until they're about ½" thick; set aside on waxed paper in 2 rows of 4. Place some crumbled blue cheese on the center of 4 of the patties; place some grilled onions on top of that; and top the patties with the remaining 4, sealing the edges together well by pinching lightly.

Lightly grease a large, heavy skillet with olive oil or Pam and place on medium-high heat. Gently place the patties, evenly spaced, into the pan and cook for 3–5 minutes each side, or until the filling feels soft when gently pressed with a spatula, and the meat is no longer red when you peek at it.

Makes 4 double or 8 single burgers.

Now Serving:

Serve on a toasted bun with lettuce, tomato, crisscrossed bacon slices and, if you're out of your mind, a few avocado slices. See you when you get back to Earth.

The Skinny:

Omit everything but the lettuce. Just joking. Okay, just ditch the bun and bacon and serve the patty on crisp lettuce with sliced tomatoes. Add a scoop of cottage cheese and it's a great protein meal. Mmm!

Can't Beet It Patty

Stuff You Need:

1 lb. finely ground sirloin

1 egg yolk

¼ cup cream

1 tsp. salt

¼ tsp. pepper

1 cup canned shoestring red beets, minced

½ an onion, minced

2 heaping Tbsp. of capers

1 Tbsp. butter

Hit It:

In a medium-size mixing bowl, mix together the ground beef, egg, cream, salt, and pepper with clean hands. Add minced beets, onions, and capers. Form 6 patties, but don't flatten them too much. Sauté in butter until golden brown on both sides and cooked through. Serve with **Dill-Mustard Sauce** and **Special Toast.**

Makes 6 burgers.

Dill-Mustard Sauce

Stuff You Need:

¼ cup honey mustard

1 tsp. French's yellow mustard

¼ cup sour cream

⅛ cup mayonnaise

1 Tbsp. dried dill

½ tsp. sea salt (it's very fine)

Hit It:

Mix all ingredients in a bowl and chill for at least one hour to let the flavors "marry."

Makes just over ½ cup.

Special Toast

Stuff You Need:

6 pieces Swedish or
   Russian rye bread

2 Tbsp. butter

Sprinkle of dried dill

Dash of onion powder

Hit It:

Melt the butter in a small dish; add a sprinkle of dried dill and a dash of onion powder. Brush some of the mixture on each piece of toast. Place under the broiler or in a toaster oven on broil until it starts to sizzle. Immediately place a hamburger patty on top. Serve with a wedge of romaine lettuce and a big tablespoon of the delicious **Dill-Mustard Sauce** on top, and savor the flavor!

Serves 6.

Now Please Pass the Panini
(with the Besto Pesto Mayo)

I first discovered panini when Rob and I were on our honeymoon in Italy. We <u>really</u> enjoyed the fine cuisine of the land. We traveled by bus to 13 cities in 16 days, and I had almost a panini a day. The ham-and-cheese ones are heavenly. Oh Lord! The fresh olive oil! The spices! I couldn't believe it. I was in love—and I don't just mean with Rob. Now, I know a panini a day keeps the buttonhole on your pants away, but I still need to have a taste now and then. You should, too.

Stuff You Need:

4 slices of white bread (pan rustica, ciabatta, or sourdough work best)

2 cooked (grilled or baked) chicken breasts

8 thin strips of roasted red peppers (bottled)

3–4 oz. imported Italian fontina cheese, Gruyère, or provolone

Olive oil or butter

Besto Pesto Mayo:

½ cup mayonnaise

1 heaping Tbsp. basil or sun-dried tomato pesto

1 tsp. regular sour cream

Hit It:

Mix the ingredients in the pesto mayo together well. Take each slice of bread, coat the outside with olive oil or butter, and coat the inside with a thin layer of the mayo. On top of one of the slices of bread, place a slice of cheese; on another, place the strips of red pepper, followed by the chicken breast.

Press both slices together, thus making a sandwich; place in a panini maker (Krups makes a good one) or sandwich presser, or on a grill pan weighted with a smaller, heavier pan on top (with this last method, you'll need to flip the sandwich).

Grill or cook sandwich until the cheese melts and both sides of the bread are golden brown and marked by the grill.

Serves 2.

Now Serving:

Add some pesto mayo on the side, along with some Fuji apple slices or little sour pickles. If you want to go wild, also serve with the onion soup on page 46 or the corn-tomato bisque on page 45.

The Skinny:

Pluck some of the bread out of each slice, which will diminish some of the calories. Or slice each piece of the bread thinner to get rid of an inch or so of bread—you can save some carbs that way. You can also use low-fat cheeses, skip the butter and mayo, and just slightly brush the bread with olive oil.

You'll Need a Napa After This Lunch
(Wine-Country Baguette)

Stuff You Need:

½ cup butter

1 Tbsp. grainy mustard

1 Tbsp. poppy seeds

1 crusty sourdough batard (full-size baguette), sliced—but not all way through— every 1½"

½ lb. bacon, cooked and crumbled

1 bunch chives, minced

4 oz. dill-Havarti cheese, shredded or sliced

Hit It:

Preheat oven to 350°. In a small skillet, heat the butter, mustard, and poppy seeds until the butter foams, but doesn't brown. Spoon the mixture in between the bread sections, then gently push bacon, chives, and cheese in as well. Wrap in foil and bake for 20–30 minutes.

Serves 4–6.

Now Serving:

Serve with red grapes or slices of Fuji apples. Perfection!

Katrina's Famous Corn-Tomato Bisque

Stuff You Need:

2 ears fresh white corn, cut off the cob, or one 12-oz. bag of sweet white-corn kernels, defrosted and drained

1 can creamed corn

3 ripe tomatoes, chopped

3 Tbsp. butter

One 10.5-oz. can Rotel tomatoes

One 4-oz. can green chilis (mild)

1 small onion, chopped

½ tsp. cayenne pepper

½ tsp. black pepper

1 Tbsp. brown sugar

1 tsp. salt

1 cup tomato juice

1 cup heavy cream

1 cup chicken broth

¼ cup cornmeal

1 teaspoon dill weed

Hit It:

Melt the butter in a large Dutch oven, and sauté the onions in it at medium-high heat until translucent; add brown sugar, and caramelize for one minute. Puree half of the fresh corn kernels in a blender or food processor; add to onions, stirring to combine. Sauté for an additional 5 minutes.

Add all the remaining ingredients, and bring to a point just before boiling. Immediately reduce heat to low and either simmer for 60 minutes on low or place all ingredients in a Crock-Pot and cook on low heat for 4–6 hours. Salt and pepper to taste.

Serves 8.

Tip:

Garnish with additional sprigs of dill or chopped green onion.

Now Serving:

This is a great side with **Just for the Halibut** (page 98) or a starter for **Don't Let Your Meat Loaf** (page 88).

So Good It Will Make You Cry Onion Soup

My love for onion soup comes from my fond memories of my Grandma Audree (my dad's mom) taking our family to the Hamburger Hamlet on Doheny Drive in Beverly Hills. It was my favorite soup of all time, and I always ordered extra cheese—sometimes two slices. How do you think I got to 300 pounds? I started young.

It's not like I'm here to fatten you up, but once in a while, you need to indulge. And no worrying about onion breath!

Stuff You Need:

3 lbs. sweet onions (Vidalia or Maui)

4 Tbsp. butter

1 clove garlic, finely minced

2 Tbsp. flour

5 cups water

5 cups beef stock

1 cup dry sherry

1 Tbsp. brown sugar

1 bay leaf

1 sprig fresh thyme or ½ tsp. dried thyme

Twelve ¼" slices of French baguette
  (**Tip:** Don't try sourdough—
  it doesn't work.)

2 cups grated Gruyère or Swiss cheese

6 Tbsp. grated Parmesan cheese

Salt and pepper to taste

Chopped fresh flat-leaf parsley for garnish

Hit It:

Preheat oven to 400°. Peel the onions, slice them in half, and cut them into wafer-thin slices. This should yield 12 cups. (**Tip:** How do you cut an onion so that you don't look like you just watched *Terms of Endearment?* Well, to avoid the mascara running down your cheeks, put a piece of bread in your mouth while chopping, or wear sunglasses. The bread soaks up the fumes—it's not 100 percent tearproof, but it helps. The glasses block the fumes; plus, they make you look cool while you're cooking.)

In a large, heavy ovenproof casserole or deep skillet, heat the butter and add the onions and garlic. Cook, stirring until onions start to brown; add brown sugar, and continue stirring for 10 minutes. Sprinkle with salt and pepper. Put the casserole in the oven and bake for 15 minutes.

After you've removed the dish from the oven, sprinkle the onions with flour, stirring to coat the pieces thoroughly. Add the water, beef stock, and sherry, and cook on the stove on high heat, scraping the bottom and sides of the pan to remove all the tasty bits. Add the bay leaf and thyme and simmer for 30 minutes, stirring frequently.

Meanwhile, place the bread on a baking sheet and bake at 400° until brown and crisp; set aside. Increase oven temp 450°. Fill 6 individual ovenproof soup tureens or deep bowls with soup; place 2 slices of toast on each bowl, sprinkle with the Gruyère and the Parmesan. Place tureens on a baking sheet or jelly-roll pan. Bake for about 10 minutes, or until the soup is hot and bubbling and the cheese is brown on top. Sprinkle with fresh chopped parsley. (**Tip:** Warn guests by saying, "I know it smells great, but if you eat this right away you're going to burn your tongue right out of your head. In other words, this is *really* hot!" Know in your heart that even after you've delivered this warning, they won't be able to wait long.)

Serves 6 as a main dish, or 12 sides.

Carnie Aside-a:

Although I love this for lunch with a salad, keep in mind that it's also a great appetizer when you have company.

Rob's Mom's Split-Pea Soup

I was in the mood to make soup one day, so I asked my husband, "Should I make a corn chowder?"

"Corn again?" Rob said, sounding like he had another plan in mind. "Honey, all I want is my mom's split-pea soup."

And here's why. (There's nothing like the real thing, baby!)

Stuff You Need:

1 pkg. (16 oz.) dry, split green peas, rinsed

6 cups water

1 cup chicken broth

2 whole bay leaves

1 tsp. Mrs. Dash (original blend)

½ tsp. pepper

1 celery stalk, finely chopped

1 carrot, finely chopped

1 medium to large onion, finely chopped

One 3-lb. can low-sodium chicken broth

2 smoked ham hocks or ham shanks

1 Tbsp. fresh thyme sprigs
   (optional for garnish)

Salt

Hit It:

Bring the first 6 ingredients to a boil; simmer for 1 hour. Add the celery, carrot, onion, chicken broth, and ham hocks or shanks; salt to taste. Simmer, stirring occasionally, until peas are cooked down, which should take about 4 hours.

Remove the shanks—strip off the meat, chop, and put back into the soup. Let it cool, and skim off the fat. Add more water if needed. Call Rob to the table immediately.

Serves 8.

Now Serving:

Serve with a piece of toasted, buttered French bread and a green salad.

Grandma Mae's Chicken Soup with Matzo Balls
(aka The Remedy)

Everyone always says that their grandma made the best chicken soup in history. Well, I have to go on the record to say that's a huge lie. <u>My</u> grandma made soup that was so good I can still hear my grandpa slurping it until the last drop was gone. He didn't care about the noise: slurp, slurp, really big slurp, pause, bigger slurp. It was so cute the way Irv would devour his soup. He was so focused on eating that he wouldn't even look up until he had an empty bowl. (Boy, do I miss them. I hope Grandma and Grandpa are somewhere eating a matzo ball right now, smiling, slurping, and reading this book.)

And by the way, there is no medicine that even begins to compare, or comfort food that can even come close, to chicken soup with matzo balls. It has the power to make us feel like we're all five years old again.

Grandma Mae's soup is actually different from some of the Jewish recipes in several ways. Start with the idea that you <u>do not</u> chop up veggies into little 1" pieces and turn them into mush—you put in huge pieces, which you strain later to extract their juices. You also cover the soup and let it simmer for 3 hours to let the flavors combine. It's absolutely delish.

Making this soup fills my kitchen with a smell that reminds me of Grandma Mae. I don't know why, but when I'm cooking it, I just naturally find myself calling my mom. In a sweet, almost wistful voice, I'll say, "I'm making her soup."

One note: This is a Skinny dish because there's not much fat in it. In fact, if you put the soup in the fridge, let it chill, and then remove the fat that's floated to the top, you're virtually gunk free. Another little tip from Mae. (Thanks, Grandma.)

I'm sure she'd be happy to know that the last time I made her soup, my hubby and I ate it for three days. I made a mental note that on one of the days, Rob actually ate it for breakfast, lunch, and dinner. Meanwhile, it made me feel full, warm, and loved. And when I had hernia surgery last year, it was better than the morphine and Advil they gave me. I think it would also help pull anyone out of a depression caused by job woes or romantic breakups. This isn't medically proven, but I have a hunch. . . .

Now, as for the matzo balls, these puppies are dense and full of flavor—just the way I love them. Grandma used real chicken fat, which was the secret ingredient. I know, I know, the stuff is like kryptonite today, but every once in a while you can live on the edge. However, if you want to go Skinny, you can use low-sodium chicken broth out of the can and omit the chicken fat. Grandma will forgive you.

P.S. Even though this is in the lunch chapter, I also love to serve it for dinner or as an appetizer.

Stuff You Need:

2 medium onions or 1 very large one, halved

2 large tomatoes, halved

4–5 large carrots, halved

5 stalks celery with the tops, cut into quarters

1 chicken, including the gizzards (but not the liver), necks, and pupiks. (**Huh?** A *pupik* is the Jewish way of saying "the innards that you find in those little plastic bags inside your chickens." You can use what you want—it's up to you. I know it grosses some people out, but it sure adds taste.)

1 turkey part (it can be a wing, neck, or leg—it's up to you)

1 beef bone (optional)

1½ tsp. salt

½ tsp. pepper

1 Tbsp. parsley flakes

7–8 chicken bouillon cubes

Hit It:

Put the turkey and chicken parts into a large pot; add the onions, carrots, tomatoes, and celery. Fill the pot with water to ½" from the top. Boil uncovered for about 45 minutes, then cover and leave on low heat for approximately 3 hours.

Take all the veggies out (except for a few pieces of carrots, celery, and onion) and put them into a strainer after they're cooked. Afterward, take a potato masher and go to town on these babies, while keeping the strained juice on the side. If you do this right, you'll end up with an orange pasty substance that you plop right back into the soup.

Throw away what you don't use or toss it into your garden.

Makes 1 huge pot of soup.

Carnie Aside-a:

I've made a few additions to this family gem over the years. For instance, a little sprinkle of parsley or cilantro just throws it over the edge. I've even had the guts to add a few garlic cloves and a parsnip, but maybe I was having a day of total empowerment—or I lost my head. Either explanation is fine because these add-ons just made the soup better and gave it a little tang. Try your own experiment!

Matzo Balls

Stuff You Need:

½ tsp. salt

¼ tsp. pepper

3 cups Matzo Meal

6 large eggs, beaten

1 Tbsp. chicken fat (very important—
Grandma's secret—don't skimp)

Seven 14-oz. cans chicken broth (only one is for the
matzo-ball mixture, the rest is to boil in)

Hit It:

Add the Matzo Meal to the eggs, then add in one can of the chicken broth. Mix until it's a doughy consistency; add chicken fat, salt, and pepper. Mix well, then form into balls about 2" in sizes. (**Tip:** Keep a dish of water in front of you and keep your hands wet while making balls. It's easier. It also helps to make sure that your hands are always moist when working with this kind of substance. Some of my fondest memories are of standing on a little step stool and watching Grandma wet her fragile, but strong, hands.)

Boil the remaining 6 cans of broth and drop the balls into it. Cover for approximately 25 minutes or longer, keeping the flame on medium heat. When the balls have floated up to the top, they're ready to rock. Oy, they're great!

Makes about 20 balls.

Bagel Crisps
(A Fab Creation to Serve with the Soup)

Stuff You Need:

4 plain bagels

¼ cup olive oil

2 cloves garlic, minced

Sea salt or Lawry's Seasoned Salt

Hit It:

Preheat the oven to 325°. With a sharp knife, carefully slice the bagels as thinly as possible, getting 6 slices per bagel. (**Tip:** I use an oven mitt on one hand; this way, I make sure I still have all my fingers when I'm done.) Spread in a layer on a cookie sheet covered with foil. Heat the oil in a small saucepan over medium heat; after about a minute, add the garlic and sea salt (or Lawry's) to taste. Set aside to cool for 10 minutes.

With a pastry brush, lightly brush the oil on both sides of the bagel crisps. Bake until golden brown (about 6 minutes); turn and bake on the second side until crisp (this should take about 5 minutes). Remove from the oven and cool.

Makes approximately 24 chips.

Gloria's Butter-You-Up Butternut-Squash Soup

This absolutely incredible recipe is from my friend Gloria Felix. She's a rockin' chef and was gracious enough to let me include it in my book. Thanks, Doggie!

Stuff You Need:

2 cups peeled and seeded
   butternut squash, chopped

1 cup peeled and seeded
   butternut squash, diced

½ cup orange juice

½ cup dark brown sugar

1 cinnamon stick

¼ cup sweet butter

1 cup leeks, chopped (white
   part only)

½ cup onions, chopped

1 Granny Smith apple, peeled,
   cored, and chopped

4 cups chicken stock
   (you may also use
   vegetable bouillon)

⅓ cup heavy cream (optional)

¼ cup extra-virgin olive oil

⅛ cup Italian parsley

½ cup canola oil

Sage oil and leaves

Salt

Freshly ground white pepper

Hit It:

Preheat oven to 450°. In a large bowl, toss the 2 cups of chopped squash with the orange juice, brown sugar, and a cinnamon stick. Pour into a roasting pan, cover with aluminum foil, and bake for an hour or until tender. Discard the cinnamon stick, drain, and set juice aside. Take a breath.

Place the butter, leeks, onions, and apple in a heavy-bottom stockpot and cook slowly over a medium flame, stirring frequently until very tender. Add chicken stock or vegetable bouillon and bring to a low boil. Add the squash, but not its juice; cook for 5 minutes. Add the heavy cream (if you want) and simmer for about 5 minutes. Cool and puree with a hand blender until very smooth. Take another breath.

Add the olive oil in a nonstick sauté pan and turn on a high flame. When the oil begins to smoke, add the 1 cup of diced squash and stir well. Add the reserved juice from the squash that was made earlier; cook until all the liquid evaporates and the squash is lightly glazed. Ladle the soup into 8 warm bowls; sprinkle the glazed, diced squash evenly over the bowls and drizzle about 1 tsp. sage oil over each. Lay 1 sage leaf on each bowl and serve immediately.

Serves 8.

Now Serving:

Add freshly chopped parsley and toasted pumpkin seeds; you can also drizzle with crème fraîche. This makes a really nice appetizer on Thanksgiving.

CHAPTER FOUR

Appetizers—A Little Goes a Long Way

We like appetizers for one major reason: They give us an excuse to eat before we really eat, and they also take the guilt away—we're talking big on taste, small on portions.

Some people enjoy appetizers more than the main dish. And for cooks, they're a great way to get creative because those tiny bites always put a smile on everyone's face. I like to describe appetizers as "cute and schnooky." Hey, I don't care if *schnooky* isn't a word you hear every day—the term perfectly describes my love for cute little things. For example, my dog Sammy is the schnookiest!

Think of appetizers this way: What else do you really need in life or on your plate but a great start and a big finish? (Hang on, the dessert chapter is coming up. . . .)

Getta Some Bruschetta

Tomato, basil, and garlic . . . oh my. You and your partner better eat these in unison because we're talking major garlic breath, but it is sooo worth it. My regular bruschetta is also featured on page 98, which I like to serve with salmon. But the little toasts here make a great appetizer.

Bruschetta with Creamy Zucchini Puree

Stuff You Need:

¼ cup extra-virgin olive oil
(plus some for drizzling)

¼ small onion, chopped

2 medium zucchini, coarsely sliced

2 Tbsp. heavy whipping cream

2 garlic cloves, minced

8 fresh basil leaves

2 Tbsp. Italian parsley

6 thick slices Italian country bread

1–2 whole peeled garlic cloves, cut in half

6 sun-dried tomatoes in oil, julienned

Salt and freshly ground pepper

Hit It:

Sauté the onions in the olive oil over medium-low heat until very soft. Add the zucchini, garlic, basil, and parsley, and sauté (covered) over medium heat. Stir occasionally until the zucchini completely falls apart, which should take about 12 minutes. Stir in the whipping cream, and salt and pepper to taste with the heat still on. Stir until the mixture becomes a slightly chunky puree; keep warm.

Lightly toast or grill the bread slices until golden on both sides. Rub each slice on one side with the garlic clove and drizzle with some olive oil on top (about a teaspoon per slice). Spread ⅙ of the puree on each slice, topping with sun-dried tomatoes. This recipe is different, but so yummy!

Makes 6 individual toasts.

Butternut Bruschetta

Stuff You Need:

1 large butternut squash, cut in half lengthwise with seeds removed

2 Tbsp. garlic, minced

3 Tbsp. melted butter

1 Tbsp. good port

4 oz. cream cheese, softened

1½ cups freshly grated Parmesan cheese, divided

1 Tbsp. brown sugar

¼ tsp. nutmeg

2 tsp. fresh sage, chopped

2 tsp. fresh parsley, chopped

2 tsp. fresh thyme, chopped

½ cup toasted walnuts, chopped

1 baguette, cut into thin slices

½ cup extra-virgin olive oil

Salt

Hit It:

Place squash, cut side down, in a 13" x 9" baking dish. Bake uncovered at 350° for one hour or until squash is tender; remove the pulp from the rind and place in a mixing bowl. Sauté garlic in butter over medium heat until soft and lightly browned for about 8 minutes; add to squash pulp in bowl. Add the port, cream cheese, brown sugar, nutmeg, sage, parsley, thyme, and ½ cup of the Parmesan to bowl; blend with a fork until smooth, and then gently fold in the walnuts. Keep near the warm stove, but don't directly heat.

Place the bread slices on a large baking sheet and brush the olive oil over them. Sprinkle with salt and bake at 400° for 4 minutes (it will probably take 2 rounds of toasting, or else use 2 baking sheets simultaneously). Sprinkle the baguette slices with the remaining 1 cup of Parmesan; bake 3–4 more minutes or until the cheese melts. Spoon the squash mixture onto each toast round, and garnish with herbs and/or chopped walnuts. Serve while slightly warm.

Makes about 2 dozen little toasts.

Tip:

Small sprigs of fresh thyme and rosemary also make a great garnish.

TUNA TARTARE

Tuna Tartare

This great recipe from my friend and wonderful chef Gloria Felix will melt in your mouth. It's so elegant and scrumptious that I wish I could eat it every other day (I sure did miss it while I was pregnant!).

Stuff You Need:

½ lb. sashimi-grade ahi tuna, finely diced

1 Tbsp. soy sauce

½ tsp. sesame oil

1 Tbsp. scallions, chopped

1 Tbsp. chives, chopped

¼ head Napa cabbage, finely shredded

½ of an avocado, peeled, seeded, and cut into quarters lengthwise

Four to six 1" wonton wrappers

1 cup olive oil

¼ tsp. black sesame seeds, toasted (for garnish)

¼ tsp. fresh ginger, finely diced (for garnish)

Hit It:

In a bowl, combine the tuna, soy sauce, sesame oil, and scallions; set aside in the fridge. Now prepare the wonton wrappers by heating the olive oil in a small stockpot. Add the wonton wrappers and cook until golden brown. Remove and set on a paper towel to cool.

Sambal Mayo

Stuff You Need:

1 egg yolk

2 tsp. lemon juice

8 oz. olive oil

⅛ tsp. salt

4 Tbsp. sambal oelek (found in most Asian markets)

2 tsp. Tabasco sauce

Hit It:

Place the egg yolk in a medium bowl and whisk until thick. Add the lemon juice and whisk to combine. Carefully add the oil in a slow stream, and whisk vigorously until well combined and slightly thickened. Add the salt, sambal, and Tabasco, and put this baby in the fridge until you're ready to use it.

Now Let's Assemble the Whole Thing

Place a wonton wrapper in the center of a plate. Mix ¼ cup Napa cabbage with 1 Tbsp. **Sambal Mayo;** place on top. Place some avocado in a pinwheel pattern on top of that; finally, place 4 Tbsp. of the tuna-tartare mixture on top of the avocado. Garnish with fresh ginger, chopped scallions, and toasted black sesame seeds. Drizzle **Sambal Mayo** across the top. You did it!

Serves 4–6.

DEVILED EGGS

Wassup with Wasabi? Deviled Eggs

This is unbelievable and so simple. Thanks to my incredible friend Katrina!

Stuff You Need:

1 dozen eggs, hard-boiled and peeled

⅔ cup wasabi mayonnaise. This is available prepared in a light version by French's, or you can add 1 tsp. wasabi paste to 1 tsp. onion juice and ⅔ cup mayo. (**Tip:** You don't have to add that much wasabi because this stuff is hot. Do a little test here to suit your taste buds.)

1 Tbsp. chives, finely minced

½ tsp. lemon juice

Paprika for garnish

Hit It:

Gently halve the eggs lengthwise and use the tip of a teaspoon to pop out the yolk into a small mixing bowl. Try not to tear the whites of the eggs, and set them in a deviled-egg plate if you own one—I don't (*hint, hint:* Mom, Wendy, anyone), so I put them on a small round platter in concentric circles. Mix together all of the remaining ingredients with the removed egg yolks; blend thoroughly until no lumps remain. Salt to taste.

If you have a pastry bag, great! Use a medium serrated tip. If you don't, no prob: Take a large Ziploc bag and cut off one of the bottom corners about ½" from the bottom, preferably with pinking shears. (**Major Tip:** Don't cut the bag until the mixture is in it or it's a huge mess.) Place the egg-filling mixture as far down into the bag as you can, trying to get it all off the spoon. When it's all in the bag, use your left hand (assuming that you're right-handed) to hold the tip of the bag and use your right hand to tightly grasp the top of it. While using your left hand to guide the tip, twist the top of the bag with your right hand, using the pressure you create within the bag to force the egg mixture through the tip into the egg whites. As the "crater" of the egg white begins to fill up, press down lightly and quickly with the tip and draw the egg mixture up into a little point like the tip of a frozen-yogurt cone. Repeat until all of the egg halves are full.

Makes 24 egg halves.

Now Serving:

Sprinkle paprika and chives over the eggs as a pretty, contrasting garnish. And watch the men in your life lose their minds over this one.

911 Moment!

If you mess one up, just spoon out the filling, eat it, wash the spoon, and refill that egg from the bag. No biggie.

ROBIN'S HOT MEAT

Robin's Hot Meat

This is a divine appetizer from my friend Robin. It's so simple, but oh so tasty.

Stuff You Need:

1 large kosher salami, Sinai brand
(Costco also has some good ones)

1 small jar apricot jam

1 jar Best Foods Honey Mustard

Hit It:

Preheat oven to 350°. In a small mixing bowl, combine the jam and mustard. Score the salami lengthwise and then crosswise about halfway deep; brush it with the jam-and-mustard mixture, fully coating it. Place the salami on a small baking pan and bake for 25 minutes. Keep reapplying the basting mixture at 25-minute intervals until the salami has cooked for about 3 hours, or until it's brown and caramelized. Gene! Thanks, Robin!

Wrap Yourself Around Your Date (Bacon-and-Almond-Wrapped Dates)

My Greek friend Vasili served these at a party once, and I was so impressed that I demanded the recipe before I walked out the door. This is a unique treat to feed your guests, and it's really easy to make. For something so small, these guys are sure packed with flavor. Thanks, Vasili—I love you!

Stuff You Need:

10 slices bacon, cut in half crosswise

20 dates, pitted

20 whole almonds, blanched
(without the brown skin)

20 sandwich toothpicks (**Tip:** Sandwich toothpicks are 3½" long and are much stronger than what you'd normally use around your home. This particular type of toothpick can be found in stores that supply products to the food-service industry.)

Hit It:

Stuff each date with an almond. Wrap a slice of bacon around each date, placing a toothpick through the center to hold it together. Place on a foil-lined baking sheet and broil until the bacon is browned (be sure that you brown all sides). Remove the toothpicks, place on a garnished tray, and serve warm.

Makes 20 dates.

Don't Mean to Boast about This Pink Toast
(Sun-Dried Tomato and Goat Cheese)

Help me—there's finally a dish that's delicious <u>and</u> pink!

This is a great appetizer for get-togethers. And if you have some with a glass of good red vino, we're talking eating euphoria.

Stuff You Need:

1 loaf French bread

6 Tbsp. butter

1 Tbsp. sun-dried tomato pesto

Garlic powder to taste

1 Tbsp. dried basil

1 Tbsp. parsley, chopped

6 oz. goat cheese (at room temp.)

Hit It:

Turn on the broiler. Mix the butter, pesto, garlic powder, basil, and parsley in a bowl. Slice the bread into ¼" slices, spread mixture on top, and broil until slightly brown. Spread the goat cheese on top and broil for one more minute. Sprinkle with parsley, and eat a few toasts before anyone notices. Rearrange the plate so that there aren't any holes in the presentation.

Makes 12–14 toasts.

Carnie Aside-a:

Sun-dried tomato pesto is pretty easy to find at your grocery store. Check out a few brands to see what suits your tastes. I guarantee that most of the prepared ones are yummy.

Give 'em the Good Stuff
(Stuffed Cherry Tomatoes with Shrimp)

Here's a great little but impressive appetizer. . . . My hat's off, as always, to Katrina.

Stuff You Need:

3 dozen cherry tomatoes

16 oz. cream cheese (at room temp.)

¼ cup mayonnaise

¼ cup sour cream

Juice of 1 lemon

½ tsp. Worcestershire sauce

Salt to taste

¼ hothouse cucumber (**Tip:** Grate through the large holes of a grater.)

⅛ cup fresh dill, minced

1 lb. small shrimp, cooked, peeled, and diced

3 Tbsp. red onion, minced

3 dashes Tabasco sauce

Minced parsley as garnish

Hit It:

Wash and dry the tomatoes; slice off a circle from the top of each (about the size of a nickel) and discard. Using a tiny spoon, scoop out the seeds; turn the shells upside down onto a paper towel on a plate and let drain completely for about 10 minutes. Set aside. Refrigerate until you're ready to use them. (**Tip:** Don't snack since you're already in the fridge. We have to keep going here!)

Put the cream cheese, mayo, and sour cream into a small mixing bowl and mix well. Add all the other ingredients except the parsley, and mix until completely blended. If you have a pastry bag, great! Use a medium serrated tip. If you don't, no prob: Take a large Ziploc bag and cut off one of the bottom corners about ½" from the bottom, preferably with pinking shears. (**Major Tip:** Don't cut the bag until the mixture is in it or it's a huge mess.) Place the shrimp mixture as far down into the bag as you can, trying to get it all off the spoon. When it's all in the bag, use your left hand (assuming that you're right-handed) to hold the tip of the bag and use your right hand to tightly grasp the top of it. While using your left hand to guide the tip, twist the top of the bag with your right hand, using the pressure you create within the bag to force the egg mixture through the tip into the tomato. As the tomato begins to fill up, press down lightly and quickly with the tip and draw the shrimp mixture up into a little point like the tip of a frozen-yogurt cone. Repeat until all of the tomatoes are full. (**Tip:** Remember my rule on messing up here—eat all the evidence of your mess and refill the bag. Oh, and wash the spoon after your snack.)

Sprinkle parsley over the tomatoes as a pretty, contrasting garnish.

Makes 3 dozen.

Olé Soufflés
(Mini Corn Mexican Soufflés)

Need I say more! Need I say anything?

Stuff You Need:

8 ears corn (with husks)

5 eggs, separated

A pinch of salt

½ cup heavy cream

¼ cup mozzarella cheese, shredded

½ tsp. baking powder

½ tsp. dried oregano

¼ cup crumbled cotija cheese
(**Huh?** Cotija is a gene Mexican cheese that's white and heavenly. I also love it on casseroles. You can substitute feta cheese if you're too far from the border to find it at the market.)

1 tsp. fresh cilantro, chopped

Hit It:

Preheat oven to 350°. Get those kernels off the cob. (**Tip:** Pull the husk back from each ear and use the husk—minus the stringy "silk"—as a handle. Hold the ear with the pointed end pressed down against the bottom of a wide bowl as you scrape the kernels off, going from the husk end to the tip with a small, sharp knife.) Separate the eggs and place the yolks in a blender; add cream and salt and pulse (blend lightly). Add the corn kernels and pour any corn "milk" from the bowl into the mixture in the blender and puree until mostly smooth, with bits of corn still visible. This should take about 30 seconds.

Using a hand mixer, beat the egg whites in a large bowl to form soft peaks. Gently fold the blended-corn mixture into the egg whites and lightly mix in the cheese, baking powder, and oregano. Pour this mixture into 8 greased-and-floured 4-oz. custard cups or mini-soufflés (or a mini-muffin pan, using 16 of the muffin cups). Bake the 4-oz. cups for 30 minutes in a water bath; for the mini-muffins, bake 20 minutes. (**Huh?** A *water bath* means that you put the dish itself inside of another dish that has about 1–2" water in it. The original dish will rest right in the water as it cooks, and that keeps it moist.)

Makes 16 mini-soufflés, or 8 larger servings.

Now Serving:

"Unmold" the soufflés onto individual plates or one large platter and garnish with crumbled cotija cheese and fresh chopped cilantro.

Chicken Wings
for My Sweetie

Inspired by Chef Paul Prudhomme, this dish is great for parties.

Stuff You Need:

16 chicken wings

4 Tbsp. unsalted butter

¼ cup onions, finely chopped

2 tsp. garlic, minced

½ cup dry sherry

2 Tbsp. soy sauce

½ cup chicken stock

½ cup honey (Hey, stop eating it out of the
    bottle . . . and stop squeezing it directly on
    your tongue, too. I can see you doing it!)

2 drops toasted sesame oil

Seasoning:

1½ tsp. ground ginger

¾ tsp. paprika

1¼ tsp. salt

¾ tsp. onion powder

¼ tsp. dry mustard

¼ tsp. cayenne pepper

½ tsp. ground sage

¼ tsp. garlic powder

¼ tsp. ground cumin

2 Tbsp. freshly minced cilantro

Hit It:

Preheat broiler. In a small bowl, combine the seasoning ingredients, which make about 2 Tbsp. Sprinkle 1 Tbsp. over the wings, and massage it in really well. Melt the butter in a heavy 12″ skillet over high heat; when it's sizzling, add the wings. Brown them on one side, turn them over, and then add the onions and garlic. Cook the wings until they're browned on both sides, which should take about 10 minutes. Now add the sherry, soy sauce, chicken stock, cilantro, and the remaining seasoning mix; bring to a rolling boil. Remove from heat and stir in the honey; let sit for 3 minutes.

Remove the wings from the sauce with tongs and place them on a broiler pan in a single layer. Broil, turning once, until brown and crispy (approximately 2 minutes each side). Watch carefully because these babies burn up quickly.

Makes 16 wings.

Now Serving:

Pour the sauce into a bowl to serve with the wings—enjoy! You can also sprinkle 1 Tbsp. cilantro on top for a yummy and pretty garnish. Try it, you'll love it.

How Swedish It Is Meatballs

How comforting! How delicious! How about right now?

Stuff You Need:

1½ lbs. ground beef

¼ lb. ground pork

1 egg, lightly beaten

1 cup milk

½ cup fine dry bread crumbs

¼ cup onions, finely chopped

3 Tbsp. butter

1½ tsp. salt

½ tsp. pepper

¼ tsp. ground nutmeg

⅛ tsp. ground allspice

¼ tsp. plus ½ tsp. dried dill

2 Tbsp. all-purpose flour

1 cup hot water

¾ cup half-and-half

8 oz. sour cream

½ Tbsp. beef-broth flavor base
   (I like Better than Bouillon paste)

Fresh dill sprigs for garnish

Hit It:

Combine the beaten egg, milk, and bread crumbs. (**Tip:** Let stand for 5 minutes. Go walk the dog—but be sure to wash your hands when you come back!) Sauté the onions in 1 Tbsp. of the butter until light golden in color. Combine the egg mixture with the onions, ground beef and pork, salt, pepper, nutmeg, allspice, and ¼ tsp. of the dried dill. Mix with your hands until smooth, and shape into 36 meatballs (about 1" in diameter). Brown meatballs in the remaining 2 Tbsp. of butter until they're really golden; pour off all but about 1 Tbsp. excess fat. Sprinkle meatballs with flour and shake the skillet. Add the hot water, stirring to loosen browned bits, and blend well. When the mixture is simmering, gently stir in the beef base. Cover and simmer for 35–40 minutes.

Add the half-and-half to the sour cream in a medium mixing bowl slowly while whisking. Add the other ½ tsp. of the dried dill, and salt and pepper to taste. Spoon this mixture onto the meatballs and heat through. Serve in a chafing dish or on a warmed platter.

Makes about 3 dozen; serves 12–18 people as an appetizer, or 6 for dinner.

Now Serving:

Garnish with fresh dill sprigs as an appetizer; these may also be served as an entrée with hot buttered egg noodles, which are tossed with 1 Tbsp. poppy seeds. No matter how you dish it up, watch everyone smile.

Carnie Aside-a:

You can put these meatballs in a Crock-Pot, bring them to a party, and keep them on low for the night.

Crescent Mooooons
(Mini Beef Pies)

I can't wait to make these for my baby nephews Leo and Beau . . . when they get a few teeth. Until then I'll just make this dish and taste-test it for them to make sure that it's more than perfect when they get older. What can I say? I'm just that kind of caring aunt!
P.S. If you eat one with a salad, you're not doing too badly in the calorie department either.

Stuff You Need:

1 pkg. Pillsbury refrigerated crescent rolls

2 Tbsp. extra-virgin olive oil

1½ cup onions, finely chopped

1 lb. lean ground beef, minced

½ cup mushrooms, sautéed, finely chopped, and patted dry with a paper towel

3 Tbsp. tomato paste

1 tsp. superfine sugar

1 tsp. ground cumin

1 tsp. sweet paprika

¼ tsp. cayenne pepper

1 Tbsp. fresh parsley, minced

¼ cup sour cream

1 egg yolk

2 Tbsp. water

¼ cup grated Parmesan cheese

Hit It:

Heat the olive oil in a nonstick frying pan over medium heat. Add the onions, stirring constantly until golden (it should take about 5–7 minutes). Add the meat, tomato paste, sugar, cumin, paprika, cayenne pepper, and salt to taste. Break up the meat with the back of a spoon as much as possible while cooking over high heat; stir constantly for about 5 minutes, or until all the pink color is gone. Remove from heat and let cool to room temperature; stir in the parsley. Add the sour cream and stir until mixed well.

Meanwhile, combine the egg yolk and water and blend well with a fork. After you've cut out 2 sheets of wax paper, gently remove the crescent-roll dough from the can. Unroll the dough onto one sheet of the paper; one at a time, separate a triangle of dough from its siblings and place on the other sheet. Take 1 Tbsp. of the meat mixture and place it in a line at the base of the triangle, leaving ½" of room around it. With 2 fingers, pick up the dough at the base of the triangle. Pull it over the filling, jelly-roll style, until you reach the tip; gently bend into a crescent shape and place on an ungreased cookie sheet. Repeat for each crescent. With a pastry brush, lightly coat each crescent on the top with the egg wash; sprinkle with Parmesan. Bake at 425° for 15–18 minutes or until golden brown.

Makes 8.

The "It's Raining Shrimp!" Volcano

It's not as hard as you think to make a dish that looks this cool. You've just gotta make sure that the cream cheese is soft. That's the key, kids.

Stuff You Need:

16 oz. cream cheese (at room temp.)

Juice of 1 lemon

1 Tbsp. Old Bay Seasoning

1 tsp. salt

½ tsp. Worcestershire sauce

¼ cup mayonnaise

½ large red bell pepper, seeded
  and finely diced

¼ cup arugula leaves cut into a chiffonade (**Tip:**
  Twist into a cigar shape and snip crosswise with
  kitchen shears to form long, thin strips.)

1 lb. bay shrimp, cooked, cleaned, and cut into
  small pieces (reserve 5 whole shrimp for garnish)

2 Tbsp. minced chives

Hit It:

In a medium mixing bowl, blend together the first 6 ingredients, one at a time and in order, until creamy. Reserve 2 Tbsp. of red bell pepper and 10 of the longest strands of arugula; blend the rest into the mixture. Gently fold in the shrimp and chives until thoroughly incorporated. Using your hands, form the mixture into a large ball. Take a piece of plastic wrap large enough to completely line the inside of a deep, large funnel (you need one big enough to hold the entire mixture); once the wrap has been placed inside the funnel and smoothed as best as you can, push the mixture completely down into the funnel, making sure that there are no air bubbles. Smooth the bottom of the mixture until it's flat and chill in the refrigerator for at least 3 hours.

By the Way, You're Not Done.
Now It's Time to Assemble the Thing:

On a large, round platter, invert the funnel carefully and lift it off. Gently peel away the plastic wrap, leaving the mixture in a cone shape. If any of the mixture is sticking out of the top of the cone like a stem, remove it and smooth the top of the mound, forming a shallow crater on top with the bowl of a soup spoon. Using the tip of the spoon, carve shallow rivulets down the sides of the volcano, with some stopping halfway down and others continuing all the way to the bottom.

Take the reserved arugula and press one piece into each rivulet. Mound the reserved shrimp into the crater on top of the mold. (**Tip:** It's cool if some fall off.) Sprinkle the reserved diced red pepper over the top and sides of the volcano, and dust some paprika unevenly down the sides of the cone. Serve surrounded with water crackers or corn chips. It's original and way cool!

Serves approximately 10.

BLA (Bacon, Lettuce, Avocado) Stuffed Tomatoes

These are adorable, and a carb-free BLT. They also look as good as they taste.

Stuff You Need:

3 dozen ripe Campari tomatoes or very large cherry tomatoes—about 3 lbs. (**Huh?** Campari tomatoes are small sweet, round, vine-ripened red tomatoes that are perfect for appetizers)

2 lbs. thinly sliced bacon, cooked extra crisp, blotted on paper towels, and crumbled; or 3 pkgs. (20 slices each) of thin, precooked bacon, microwaved until crisp, blotted on paper towels, and crumbled

1 ripe avocado, diced into ½" pieces and lightly tossed with the juice of half a lemon

⅛ head iceberg lettuce, finely shredded (about 1 cup)

½ cup white Vermont cheddar cheese, finely shredded

⅛ cup Best Foods mayonnaise, plus a scant ⅛ tsp. of prepared wasabi (or more if you prefer spicier, but watch out—this stuff is atomic) or ⅛ cup prepared wasabi mayonnaise (Trader Joe's is excellent but extra spicy; for a lighter version, you can substitute French's Light Wasabi Mayonnaise)

⅛ tsp. white balsamic vinegar

A pinch of sugar

Hit It:

With a sharp knife, slice off the tops of the tomatoes to provide an opening large enough to use a small teaspoon for stuffing them. Using a small spoon, scoop out the flesh and seeds from the centers, reserving about ½ cup seedless flesh. (**Tip:** Save the rest, along with the discarded tops, to make some salsa.) Chop the reserved flesh and let the shells dry upside down on paper towels. Transfer the lettuce to a medium-sized bowl; stir in the chopped tomato.

Mix together the wasabi, mayonnaise, vinegar, and sugar in a separate dish; stir gently until well blended, then toss with the lettuce mixture. Gently toss the bacon (reserving ⅛ cup) and shredded cheese in; toss in half of the diced avocado, reserving half. Place the tomatoes upright on a platter and spoon the filling into them, mounding slightly. Top with the reserved diced avocado and crumbled bacon. Serve immediately.

Serves 15–20.

Carnie's Fave Appetizers to Bring to a Party

1. **Take a Dip in the Sea Tuna Dip.** They'll flip!
2. **Bruschetta with Creamy Zucchini Puree** with toasted pita chips.
3. **Break Your Heartichoke Dip.** Bring the whole Crock-Pot with you, along with some of your favorite crackers.
4. **How Swedish It Is Meatballs.** Men will fall at your feet. Tell them to avoid ruining your pedicure.
5. A huge bowl of **Holy Guacamole.** Double the recipe. ¡Delicioso!

Holy Guacamole

This recipe makes a nice big bowl. ¡Olé!

Stuff You Need:

6 avocados

Juice of 1 lime

½ cup plus 2 Tbsp. onion, finely chopped

2 large cloves garlic, minced

2 plum tomatoes, cored, seeded, and chopped

⅓ cup cilantro leaves, chopped

1 fresh jalapeño or serrano chili, seeded and chopped (**Hint:** If you like it spicy, leave in the seeds and rind.)

2 Tbsp. jalapeño juice from the jar

Salt and pepper to taste

Hit It:

Pour the lemon or lime juice into a large bowl and add the avocados. (**Tip:** As you peel and pit the avocados, coat them in the juice so that they don't discolor.) Add the next 8 ingredients and mix together, using 2 dinner knives or a fork, until you get the desired texture. It's my opinion that this is God's creation.

Serves 12 for chip-dipping.

Rockin' Rolly Broc-a-mole

This is delish, plus you'll get your veggies in.

Stuff You Need:

½ cup frozen edamame (soybeans), shelled and blanched for 2 minutes in boiling water

1 cup broccoli stalks, peeled and blanched for 2 minutes (**Tip:** Don't overcook your broccoli—it never did anything mean to you!)

1 avocado, peeled, pitted, and diced into large pieces (**The Skinny:** You can omit the avocado if you're feeling saintly. If you do, know that I'm proud of you.)

½ red onion, finely minced

1 clove fresh garlic, minced

1 Tbsp. chopped green chilis (canned variety)

Juice of 1 lemon

½ tomato, seeded and diced

½ tsp. honey

⅛ tsp. dried oregano

Salt and pepper to taste

A dash of Worcestershire sauce

Hit It:

Puree the edamame and the broccoli in a food processor until creamy; transfer to a small mixing bowl. Cut the avocado into 1" pieces, and combine in a separate bowl with the remaining ingredients. Transfer the broccoli puree to the avocado mixture, and to everything, stir, stir, stir. (Sorry, I couldn't resist.) Take care not to blend so well that there aren't any chunks of avocado left.

Serve with raw vegetables or baked tortilla chips. Yowza!

Makes approximately 2½ cups, or an appetizer for 6.

Break Your Heartichoke Dip:
THE SINFUL

When my friend Katrina made this recipe, it really did break my heart—and I begged for the recipe. This is such an easy dish to prepare, and it makes a great potluck dish, too. I guarantee you'll scrape up every last bite. It's insanely good.

Stuff You Need:

Two 14-oz. cans quartered artichoke hearts packed in water, drained and chopped roughly into 1" pieces

Two 14-oz. cans artichoke bottoms packed in water, drained and chopped roughly into 1" pieces

1½ cups mayonnaise

1 cup sour cream

1½ cups grated Parmesan cheese (**Cheapo Tip:** Honestly, the kind in the cardboard shaker works the best!)

½ cup jack cheese

One 4-oz. can diced green chilis

2 cloves garlic, minced

1 Tbsp. lemon juice

Hit It:

Okay, this is an easy one: Just combine all of the ingredients into a Crock-Pot and cook on low for 2–3 hours or until heated through. (**Tip:** If you're short on time, you may start it at the high setting for an hour or so, but it's better to be a slowpoke here. The deal is that the longer this stays in the Crock-Pot, the spicier and better it will taste. Don't worry about leaving it on low throughout an entire evening for a party—just be careful not to leave the house. I'm always worried that if I leave for 3 seconds the entire place will be up in flames and I'll never be able to explain this to my mother, who taught me to always check 300 times to make sure that I really did unplug the curling iron . . . and the Crock-Pot.)

Makes a 5-quart Crock-Pot's worth, and serves approximately 12 people. You can even have some "big dippers" over, and you'll still have enough.

Oven Version:

If you prefer to make this in the oven, divide the recipe between two casseroles because the Crock-Pot accommodates a much larger amount of dip. Bake, uncovered, at 350° for 30 minutes or until heated through and bubbling. Don't taste it when it's this hot or you'll set your poor little tongue on fire. Plus, anything salty you eat for the next two days will kill if you burn your tongue on hot dip. Trust me.

Now Serving:

Serve immediately with chunks of country bread, regular or low-fat tortilla chips, toasted pita chips, crackers, or the **Bagel Crisps** on page 49.

Carnie Aside-a:

The leftovers make a decadent omelette filling! Oh, and after the party, you can feed the rest of the bread, chips, or crackers to the birds in your yard. It's a nice way to both support nature and not support your own noshing.

Break Your Heartichoke Dip:
THE SKINNY

The rich dip has been toned down here by substituting low-fat dairy products for the original ingredients and by serving with cooled steamed-veggie dippers and baked tortilla chips.

Stuff You Need:

Two 14-oz. cans quartered artichoke hearts packed in water, drained and chopped roughly into 1" pieces

Two 14-oz. cans artichoke bottoms packed in water, drained and chopped roughly into 1" pieces

1½ cups light mayonnaise

1 cup light sour cream

1½ cups grated fat-free Parmesan cheese (**Cheapo Tip:** Honestly, the kind in the cardboard shaker works the best!)

½ cup 2% jack or mild cheddar cheese, grated

One 4-oz. can diced green chilis

2 cloves garlic, minced

1 Tbsp. lemon juice

Hit It:

Combine all ingredients into a Crock-Pot and cook on low for 2–3 hours or until heated through. (**Tip:** If you're short on time, you may start it at the high setting for an hour or so. But the longer this stays in the Crock-Pot, the spicier and better it tastes, so don't worry about leaving it on low throughout an entire evening for a party.)

Makes a 5-quart Crock-Pot's worth, or feeds 12.

Oven Version:

If you prefer to make this in the oven, divide the recipe between 2 casseroles because the Crock-Pot accommodates a much larger amount of dip. Bake, uncovered, at 350° for 30 minutes or until heated through and bubbling.

Now Serving:

Serve immediately with lightly steamed or raw veggie dippers and baked tortilla chips. It's also good with jicama sticks and crispy rice crackers.

Carnie Aside-a:

The leftovers make a decadent omelette filling!

FROM BOTTOM TO TOP: CURRIED-AWAY TOFU DIP, TAKE A DIP IN THE SEA TUNA DIP, AND NO WORRIES SHRIMP-CURRY DIP

Take a Dip in the Sea Tuna Dip

All I can say is . . . forget about it! This is not to be believed.

Stuff You Need:

One 12-oz. can white albacore tuna
    packed in water, drained

⅜ cup mayonnaise

7 slices jarred jalapeños, roughly chopped;
    plus 1 tsp. of the juice (**Tip:** Add more or
    less depending on how spicy you like it.)

4 scallions with 1" of the green tops

½ cup sour cream

⅓ cup cilantro leaves, trimmed and packed

½ tsp. salt

⅛ tsp. pepper

Hit It:

Put all the ingredients in a food processor and pulse until smooth and creamy. Cover and stick in the fridge for an hour (or until you're ready to serve it).

Makes approximately 1½ cups, or an appetizer for 1—just kidding! Serves 6.

Now Serving:

Haul out the tortilla chips or Fritos. Ahh!

Carnie Aside-a:

I always double this recipe for a party.

Curried-Away Tofu Dip

This is really different and a major protein dish. Who knew?

Stuff You Need:

One 8-oz. carton firm silken tofu, drained

1½ tsp. kosher salt

2 Tbsp. fresh cilantro, chopped

2 Tbsp. fresh Italian parsley, minced

2 Tbsp. Madras curry powder (or the best-quality
    one you can find)

1 scallion (green and white parts), thinly sliced

2 Tbsp. mango chutney

2 Tbsp. cream cheese (at room temp.)

1 Tbsp. cashew butter

½ cup mayonnaise

2 Tbsp. lemon juice

Juice of 1 lime

A dash of steak sauce or Worcestershire

Hit It:

Add all the ingredients to a food processor and pulse until creamy and smooth. Put in the fridge for at least 1 hour (if you have the time), since it thickens perfectly as it chills.

Makes 2½ cups.

Now Serving:

Dip celery sticks, sweet red bell-pepper strips, carrot sticks, pita chips, or crackers into this yummy concoction.

No Worries Shrimp-Curry Dip

My good friend Bonnie gave me this recipe, which she got from her friends Lynne and Mort Rubenstein. They've both passed on, so this is in their honor. This recipe is absolutely beyond the beyond—watch people's faces when they eat this one!

Stuff You Need:

8 oz. cream cheese (at room temp.)

½ cup sour cream

1 Tbsp. curry powder

¼ tsp. garlic powder

¼ cup mango chutney

1 tsp. capers, drained

1 cup cooked shrimp, diced

Hit It:

Combine the softened cream cheese with the sour cream, then stir in the curry powder, garlic powder, and chutney. Fold in the capers and shrimp, and get ready to serve immediately. (If you're preparing in advance, remove from the fridge 30 minutes before serving).

Serves about 8.

Killer Diller Dip

Stuff You Need:

1 cup sour cream

1½ cups mayonnaise

2 Tbsp. dry onion flakes

2 Tbsp. dry parsley flakes

⅛ tsp. garlic powder

2 tsp. dry dill weed

1 tsp. Beau Monde seasoning
   or Lawry's Seasoned Salt

Hit It:

Mix all the ingredients together and chill for several hours.

Makes approximately 3 cups.

Now Serving:

This is great with raw veggies like broccoli, cauliflower, cucumber or sweet red bell-pepper strips, carrot and celery sticks, and cherry tomatoes. (Dare I say that it's fab with potato chips, too?) It's the perfect party dip.

Hot Chickpea Dip (Hummus)

I didn't really discover hummus until I was 25 . . . what a shame! It seems so sinful, but it's actually good for you <u>and</u> a great source of protein. Now that we've gotten that nutritional message out of the way, I'll confess that the other reason I like hummus is because it's an excuse to eat something on a piece of delicious pita bread. Hey, what am I supposed to eat it on—my hand? (Actually, I would—ha ha!)

Stuff You Need:

Two 16-oz. cans chickpeas, drained
 (reserve the juice)

3–4 cloves garlic

1½ tsp. kosher or coarse sea salt

1 cup tahini (sesame-seed paste)

½ cup (or more) lemon juice

½ cup olive oil (divided into two ¼ cups)

¼ cup flat-leaf parsley, minced

Paprika for garnish

Hit It:

Place the parsley and ¼ cup of the olive oil into a food processor and mix until smooth and green. Pour the resulting parsley oil into a glass jar or dish; cover and refrigerate until serving time. (You can actually make this mixture and let it sit and become an emerald green color several hours prior to—or even a few days before—serving.)

Drain and dry the chickpeas, reserving the juice from one can. In the food processor, pulse the garlic until finely minced, adding 1 Tbsp. chickpea juice if necessary. Add the chickpeas and continue to pulse, scraping down the sides until the mixture is a chunky puree. Add the salt, tahini, lemon juice, and the other ¼ cup olive oil; mix and then taste (my favorite part of cooking!). Add enough of the reserved chickpea juice to make a thick, creamy consistency. (**Tip:** When you press the back of a spoon into the mixture, the indentation should remain.) Taste again, and add additional lemon or salt if needed—but don't go nuts.

Makes approximately 4 cups, or an appetizer for 12.

Now Serving:

Spread onto a shallow bowl and drag the tip of a spoon lightly in a spiral over the top to leave a channel for the oil to rest in. Drizzle the hummus with parsley oil, then sprinkle with paprika.

Carnie Aside-a:

I substitute cilantro for parsley and lime juice for lemon juice, and add ½ tsp. of canned diced jalapeño peppers if I feel like being a wild woman who lives on the edge.

Crabby Crab Dip

This is a real crowd-pleaser. I swear, it's the juice at any party.

Stuff You Need:

One 6-oz. can crabmeat, or 6 oz. fresh blue crabmeat (**Tip:** Check out your meat and remove any stray shells—ick!)

8-oz. cream cheese (at room temp.)

¼ cup mayonnaise

1 Tbsp. sour cream

3 green onions, sliced (**Tip:** We want the white parts and only 1" of the green parts.)

1 large garlic clove, minced

¼ cup fresh Parmesan cheese, grated

⅛ cup white cheddar cheese, finely grated

¼ cup apple juice

2 tsp. sugar

1 tsp. ground mustard

⅓ cup sliced almonds (for garnish)

½ teaspoon freshly chopped parsley (for garnish)

Hit It:

Preheat oven to 375°. Mix the cream cheese, mayo, Parmesan cheese, white cheddar cheese, onions, garlic, apple juice, sugar, and mustard together and place in an ungreased 9" pie pan. Drain and remove any shells from the crabmeat in a strainer; break up the crab pieces and then stir them into the other ingredients. Sprinkle with the almonds. Bake uncovered for 15–20 minutes, until it's hot and bubbly. Sprinkle with parsley.

Serves 10.

Now Serving:

I like this dish with crackers, tortilla chips, or raw sliced veggies like zucchini, yellow and red sweet bell peppers, and cucumbers. Incredible, huh?

Nobody Puts Baba in a Corner:
THE SINFUL

Remember the trademark line in <u>Dirty Dancing</u>? "Nobody puts Baby in a corner," cried leather-jacket-wearing, hip-swiveling Johnny Castle, aka Patrick Swayze.

Well, no one will put this traditional Middle Eastern dish, which is full of bite and flavor, in a corner either.

Stuff You Need:

2 small eggplants (**Tip:** The way to know you're getting a good eggplant is if it's dark purple and firm to the touch. Yes, it's okay to stand in the veggie aisle and feel the stuff up.)

3 cloves garlic, minced

1½ tsp. salt

⅓ cup tahini (sesame-seed paste)

¼ cup lemon juice

⅛ cup plain nonfat yogurt

1 Tbsp. parsley, minced

Parsley sprigs for garnish

Hit It:

Halve the eggplants lengthwise, remove the stems, and place them skin-side up on a greased, foil-lined broiler pan. Broil for about 25 minutes, or until the skin is charred and the pulp inside is very soft. Remove from the broiler and cool. Gently remove the soft, cooked eggplant from the outer, charred skin; discard the skin. Place the eggplant pulp in a colander set inside a bowl in the refrigerator and chill for at least ½ hour (you can go up to several hours). Discard the juice that collects in the bowl.

Place the eggplant in a food processor or blender and pulse until pureed. Add the other ingredients one at a time, saving the lemon juice and salt for last; continue to pulse. Add the lemon juice and salt, putting in only a small amount at a time and tasting to correct the seasoning as you go. Remove from the food processor to a shallow serving platter and stir in the parsley. Garnish with parsley sprigs and serve.

Makes 2 cups, or an appetizer for 8.

Nobody Puts Baba in a Corner:
THE SKINNY

Stuff You Need:

2 small eggplants

3 cloves garlic, minced

1½ tsp. salt

3 Tbsp. tahini (sesame-seed paste)

1 tsp. olive oil

¼ cup lemon juice

⅛ cup plain nonfat yogurt

1 Tbsp. parsley, minced

Parsley sprigs for garnish

Hit It:

Halve the eggplants lengthwise, remove the stems, and place them skin-side up on a greased, foil-lined broiler pan. Broil for about 25 minutes, or until the skin is charred and the pulp inside is very soft. Remove from the broiler and cool. Gently remove the soft, cooked eggplant from the outer, charred skin; discard the skin. Place the eggplant pulp in a colander set inside a bowl in the refrigerator and chill for at least ½ hour (you can go up to several hours). Discard the juice that collects in the bowl.

Place the eggplant in a food processor or blender and pulse until pureed. Add the other ingredients one at a time, saving the lemon juice and salt for last; continue to pulse. Add the lemon juice and salt, putting in only a small amount at a time and tasting to correct the seasoning as you go. Remove from the food processor to a shallow serving platter and stir in the parsley. Garnish with parsley sprigs and serve.

Makes 2 cups, or an appetizer for 8.

CHAPTER FIVE

Evening Bliss—
Otherwise Known
As "Dinner"

Even when I was sent to bed without supper as a kid, I always found my way back into the kitchen around midnight. Let's get real: How could any of us ever really skip dinner? I'm not sure if I could make it until morning—I might starve to death. Okay, maybe I'm being a bit dramatic here, but in my mind, no dinner is a dire situation.

There are so many choices when it comes to the big meal, but here are some of my favorites. Try them yourself, or better yet, serve them to someone you love.

Chicken Cacciatore If You Can

Five weeks after my gastric-bypass surgery I wasn't eating much, and the only cooking I did was for my future husband, Rob, when he came to town. He was living in Philly and I was in Los Angeles, which was tough, but we were having a lovely long-distance romance. The only problem was that I didn't have the post-surgery energy to really go to town on the meals, although I wanted to make each visit beautiful for him.

One morning I remember following the recipe on the back of a soup can to make Rob a meal for that evening, when he'd be flying in. (It was your basic mushroom soup poured over chicken and rice.) Unfortunately, his flight was cancelled and the next one was delayed. Then they lost his luggage over Vegas and he got diverted. My poor baby finally arrived at 1 A.M. and said, "Honey, can we just go to bed? I'm not even hungry."

He never tasted a bite of the soup glop . . . maybe that was a good thing. I didn't freak out either, as women sometimes do when the guy doesn't eat after they slaved over a difficult back-of-the-soup-can recipe. Anyway, the following morning I made my future hubby pancakes with warm maple syrup. And bananas. And blueberries. And bacon. And eggs. He was so happy, and so hungry. At that point it wasn't really appropriate to whip up another chicken dish, but over the years, I've graduated from soup cans to this bad boy below. If you have an hour, I promise that this is the bomb. It truly is the way to your guy's heart. Trust me—I've seen it work time and time again on mine.

P.S. This is also my favorite cacciatore on Earth.

Stuff You Need:

1 large roasting chicken, cut up

1 thick piece of pancetta (**Huh?** Pancetta is a type of bacon), about ¹⁄₁₆ of a pound

1 cup flour, seasoned with 1 tsp. each salt, pepper, paprika, and garlic powder

¼ cup olive oil

1 yellow onion, chopped

2 cups brown mushrooms, sliced

½ of a red bell pepper, cut into strips

4 cloves garlic, finely minced

1 Tbsp. capers

1 small carrot, grated on the medium side of the grater

1 cup dry red or white wine (optional, but it makes this dish taste so good)

2 red tomatoes, chopped

1 small can tomato paste

1 cup chicken broth

¼ tsp. crushed red pepper

1½ tsp. thyme

1 bay leaf

10 large basil leaves, snipped into strips with kitchen shears

⅓ cup flat-leaf Italian parsley— half minced, half reserved for garnish

Good-quality Parmesan cheese

Hit It:

In a large covered chicken fryer, fry the pancetta in the olive oil over medium heat until brown, about 7–8 minutes. Put the seasoned flour in a paper bag and shake a couple of pieces of chicken at a time until coated. Add the chicken to the pan and brown for 4 minutes on each side; remove and set aside.

Add the onions and red bell pepper, season with salt and pepper, and sauté for 4 minutes. Add the carrots, mushrooms, capers, tomatoes, and garlic; sauté for 10 minutes. Stir in the wine and deglaze the pan by scraping up any bits stuck to the pan. Add the tomato paste a tablespoon at a time until the desired consistency is reached; bring the mixture to a boil and stir in the red pepper, bay leaf, thyme, half the parsley, and basil. Add the chicken to the mixture and reduce to medium-low heat. Simmer uncovered, stirring occasionally, for 1 hour, then taste and correct the seasoning and consistency. If it's too thick, add broth; if it's too thin, add tomato paste.

Serves 6.

Now Serving:

Scoop over my **Righteous Mashed Potatoes with Roasted Garlic** (page 108) or long egg noodles, garnishing with parsley and shaved Parmesan.

Give Your Company the Bird

This is another yummy chicken dish that I love to make because it contains avocados. That makes it healthy . . . well, almost. I do promise that it's definitely different and colorful!

Stuff You Need:

4 boneless chicken breasts, gently
   pounded on wax paper

Juice of ½ a lemon

Salt and pepper to taste

3 Tbsp. unsalted butter

¼ cup chicken stock
   (homemade is preferable,
   but low-sodium canned is okay, too)

¼ cup dry white wine

1 cup heavy cream

Some freshly grated nutmeg

⅛ tsp. cayenne pepper or paprika

8 slices avocado, but not one that's too ripe
   (**Tip:** An avocado is ripe when it yields
   to gentle pressure when squeezed gently
   in the palm of your hand. If you're not sure
   if it's ready, you can tell by pressing the stem
   end—if it's still very hard, the avocado
   isn't ready yet.)

½ cup Gruyère cheese, grated

12 slices tomato, peeled and seeded (**Tip:**
   To seed a tomato, cut it in half along the
   "equator," then use a narrow-tipped spoon
   or grapefruit spoon to scoop out the seeds
   and the yellow gelatinous substance.)

Hit It:

Lightly rub the chicken with lemon juice, then sprinkle with salt and pepper. Heat the butter in a medium to large skillet until it foams like Cujo in that scary movie. Sauté the chicken, brushing each breast a couple of times to keep it coated with butter. Cook for 7–8 minutes or until the juices run clear. (Be careful not to overcook the chicken because it will get dry and you'll cry.)

When cooked through, move the chicken to a gratin dish; add the stock and wine to the butter in the pan. (No, you can't drink it.) Over high heat, reduce the mixture until thickened. Add the cream and nutmeg; continue cooking and thickening. (**Tip:** You'll know it's thick enough if it coats the back of a spoon.) Remove from heat and season with salt, pepper, and nutmeg, to taste.

Arrange the chicken breasts, avocado, and tomato slices alternately in a nice pretty pattern. (Yes, it's even impressive looking—that's why this is a good mom-in-law dish.) In a shallow baking dish, pour most of the gene sauce in and top with cheese. Heat under the broiler until bubbly and glazed. Sprinkle a little paprika or cayenne pepper on the top.

Serves 4.

Now Serving:

Serve with a little sauce on the side for extra dipping. You can also cut the chicken breasts and fan them out for a really pretty presentation.

Perfect Breasts and Thighs
(It Only Applies to Baked Chicken—Darn!)

Finally, a reason to be happy about your thighs! If that's not something to rejoice about, then I'm not sure what else I can say. . . .

*Seriously, this is the perfect baked-chicken dish—it's so easy that you just can't lose. By the way, this is a meal that practically screams for a side of **Righteous Mashed Potatoes** (page 108) or **Oh-So-Nice Baked Rice** (page 114). You could also do a 360 on everyone and serve this chicken with the **Broc On Mold** on page 128, too. It's good to shake things up.*

Stuff You Need:

4 chicken-breast halves with skin, bone in

4 chicken thighs with skin, bone in

3 Tbsp. melted butter

1 Tbsp. sugar

2 Tbsp. salt

1 Tbsp. paprika

1 Tbsp. garlic powder

1 whole lemon

1 onion, peeled and sliced into circles

1 cup chicken broth

1 Tbsp. flour

A pinch of thyme, dried or fresh

Hit It:

Preheat oven to 375°. Coat a large roasting pan with 1 Tbsp. melted butter, arrange the onion circles on the bottom of the pan, and place the chicken pieces, skin-side up, on top of that. In a small dish or saucer mix the sugar, salt, paprika, and garlic powder; set aside.

Brush the chicken with the remaining 2 Tbsp. melted butter; cut the lemon in half and squeeze the juice over that, making sure to cover each piece. (**Tip:** Don't cut the lemon the long way, but in the way that creates a wagon-wheel pattern. Then gently rotate the tip of a sharp knife held flat around the core of the halved lemon to make sure that the seeds pop out.) Hold the dish of seasonings over the roasting pan and sprinkle it all over the chicken pieces, a pinch at a time. (Just cover those babies up; use some of the onions, too.) Bake for 50 minutes, or until the skin is as crispy as you were on your last vacation.

When the skin is browned and the juices run clear when the chicken is pricked, it's done. Remove the chicken and onions and place them on a foil-covered platter or keep warm in the oven.

Serves 4 generously.

Getting Saucy:

Skim most of the fat from the top of the pan, leaving the juices. Transfer the pan to the stove top and simmer over a medium heat. Sprinkle in the flour and stir briskly to break up any bits that are stuck to the pan. Deglaze the pan with the chicken broth, stirring briskly; add a pinch of thyme. Serve in a gravy boat with the chicken and prepare to moan

Stir-Crazy Chicken
with Broccoli

This dish is a perfectly lean lunch or dinner. It's flavorful, low in fat, high in protein, and easy to prepare. If you're looking for sauce, you won't find it here—I like it plain with side salad topped by a little ranch dressing.

Stuff You Need:

1 lb. broccoli florets, steamed
   or microwaved until bright
   green, but still a little crisp

2 cooked boneless, skinless
   chicken-breast halves,
   cut into 2" chunks

4 garlic cloves, minced

1 Tbsp. grated ginger

2 Tbsp. tamari sauce

¼ tsp. red-chili flakes

3½ Tbsp. extra-virgin olive oil

1 tsp. toasted sesame oil

Sliced scallions and
   sesame seeds (for garnish)

Hit It:

In a large, heavy frying pan or wok, heat 2 Tbsp. olive oil with the sesame oil on medium-high heat until hot. Gently toss in the chicken and stir until browned and no longer pink in the middle (this should take about 4 minutes); remove and set aside. Add the garlic, ginger, tamari, chili flakes, and the remaining olive oil; gently fold in the broccoli, cooking for 2–3 minutes or until tender. Gently fold in the cooked chicken and heat for 1 minute; remove everything from the pan and mound onto a large platter, in the center of a ring of steamed white rice that's been topped by a little butter. Garnish with sliced scallions and sprinkle with sesame seeds.

Serves 4—or 2 if you haven't eaten for a week.

The Skinny:

You can always omit the rice if your jeans are too tight. If you're feeling somewhere in the middle of carbs versus no carbs, then just eat a few teaspoons of rice with the dish. It's totally satisfying that way.

Chow Down on Tiffany's Mom's Healthy Chicken Chowder

It's really nice to use a recipe from a dear friend's mother. Let me tell you one thing about Tiffany's mom, Maureen: She's one of the classiest ladies I've ever known. So I hope she doesn't mind if I take a minute to say to everyone that her chicken chowder kicks . . . well, let's leave it there.

You can serve this dish over brown rice or noodles as the perfect antidote to a chilly day. Perhaps you could thumb through an issue of Town & Country or Robb Report while slurping, uh, I mean sipping, daintily. Do it for Maureen!

Stuff You Need:

¼ cup onion, chopped

½ tsp. curry powder

2 Tbsp. olive oil

2 Tbsp. flour

4 cups chicken broth

2 tomatoes, chopped

2 apples, pared and chopped
(**Tip:** The tart ones are best.)

½ cup carrots, sliced

¼ cup green pepper, chopped

2 Tbsp. parsley

1 Tbsp. lemon juice

1 tsp. sugar

Pepper to taste

1½ cups yellow squash,
pared and chopped

1 cup cooked chicken, diced

Hit It:

Heat the oil in a big saucepan; cook the onion in curry powder until it's tender but not brown. Stir in the flour; add the chicken broth, tomatoes, apples, carrots, green pepper, parsley, lemon juice, sugar, salt, and pepper; and make sure that everything comes to a boil (remember to stir it every now and then). Turn the heat down and let this baby simmer for 15 minutes. Add the squash and chicken; simmer for another 15 minutes, testing the squash to see when it's tender.

Serves 6.

The Skinny:

Don't add any carbs on the side.

Carnie Aside-a:

Hope that it snows later that day, because this is comfort food at its finest!

A Lotta Chicken Enchilada Casserole

Hola, amigos. This is Carnie's alter ego, Carmen Lupe Maria Sanchez Wilson. She wanted me to tell you about this muy excelente recipe from my culture. I told her, "Chica, this one is perfect if you ever get into a fight with your esposo, Rob. This is a muy bueno make-up dish!"

Carn's response: "Pass the sour cream. I want to pick a fight just so there can be some making up."

This recipe is fantastico because it's from my homeland in Mexico. It's filled with fresh ingredients and nothing is processed. It's also authentic to my heritage because it's full of fresh jalapeños, chicken, sweet yellow onions, and juicy, ripe red tomatoes. ¡Que delicioso!

Stuff You Need:

2 Tbsp. butter

1½ lbs. cooked chicken, shredded (**Tip:** You can poach chicken breasts with the bone in them in water, with a couple of chicken bouillon cubes added for flavor.)

1 small onion, chopped

3 jalapeños, diced, with seeds and membranes removed (**Huge Tip:** Don't touch your eyes . . . ouch!)

2 Tbsp. mild green chilis, chopped

½ cup half-and-half

Salt and pepper to taste

¼ tsp. garlic salt

½ tsp. dried oregano

½ tsp. paprika

3 cups Monterey jack cheese, grated

12 corn tortillas, cut into quarters (they should look like triangles)

⅔ cup cheddar or longhorn cheese

1 Tbsp. olives, chopped (plus some for garnish)

Chopped green onions for garnish

Hit It:

Preheat oven to 350°. Melt the butter in a skillet and sauté the chicken for 1 minute. Add the onion, jalapeños, and green chilis, and cook for 3 minutes; cover and set aside.

In a saucepan, heat the half-and-half; stir in the salt and pepper, oregano, paprika, and garlic salt, and bring to a slow boil. Add the chicken mixture, blend well, cover, and simmer for 2 minutes. Lightly grease a 2-quart casserole dish (8" x 8") and line with the tortilla triangles. Add a portion of the chicken over the tortillas, sprinkle with jack cheese and olives, and add another layer of tortillas. Repeat until all of the ingredients are used up. Top with cheddar cheese and bake for 35 minutes. Garnish with some olives and green onions.

Serve with sour cream, guacamole, diced fresh tomatoes, and more onions if you like. ¡Olé!

Serves 6–8.

Tip:

If you're cooking with your sweetie, give him the job of cutting up all the veggies (of course, this might not happen if you're in that fight!). Guys seem to love chopping for some reason. I don't get it—maybe it makes them think they're in the wild, hacking stuff away so that you can make it to the next field.

Carnie Aside-a:

It might seem like a better idea to buy those roasted chickens they sell in the grocery store to use in your enchiladas, but don't do it! They're usually so oversalted.

Don't Let Your Meat Loaf

So what if meat loaf has the same reputation as James Dean? It's the white T-shirt and blue jeans of food—nothing fancy, sorta street. But you know what? It's just fabulous, like a warm blanket on a cold afternoon.

One note: I hate your typical meat-loaf sandwich because I don't like cold meat—I think the meat just loses its charm in the middle of a couple slices of bread. I'd rather revive my meat loaf the next day with a little microwave warmth, and it's better than ever. In fact, if you heat it up and stick it into a French loaf with some mozzarella cheese and some tomato sauce—hello!

P.S. Pass the ketchup.

P.P.S. You must serve this with mashed potatoes and gravy. I think there's a law or something.

Stuff You Need:

⅔ lbs. of each of the following: ground chuck, lean pork, and veal, mixed together

1 cup milk

1 cup quick oats, uncooked

½ cup flat-leaf parsley, chopped

⅓ cup onion, finely chopped

1 large clove garlic, minced

¼ cup carrots, grated or shredded

1 egg

3 Tbsp. ketchup or chili sauce

1 Tbsp. horseradish

¼ cup unsweetened applesauce

⅛ tsp. allspice

1½ tsp. salt

½ tsp. pepper

For the Gravy:

1 Tbsp. flour

1 Tbsp. butter

4 Tbsp. water

Hit It:

Preheat oven to 375°. In a large bowl, mix all the ingredients thoroughly. (**Tip:** Don't be scared to dig into the meat with your hands. Just wash those mitts first and get to it. Oh, you might want to remove any good rings—no one wants to bite into a diamond chip.) Pat the mixture into a 9" x 5" loaf pan. Bake about 1 hour or until the loaf is firm and the top is browned. The juice should be clear, and a meat thermometer should read 155°. Remove from the oven and let it rest in the pan for 10 minutes before slicing.

Now it's time to make the gravy. Pour all the juices from the pan into a skillet. Add the flour, butter, and water; whisk on medium heat until thick and bubbly. (Add more water for a thinner gravy, or to yield more of it.) Whoever gets some of this gravy is very lucky. It doesn't make too much, but we have to take the good and bad in life.

Serves 6.

Now Serving:

As a starter, I love to make a simple tossed salad filled with carrots, peppers, scallions, and Thousand Island dressing (or the low-cal variety). Yum. A few steamed veggies, including a mix of zucchini, carrots, broccoli, and cauliflower, are also great as a low-cal side.

Now, I hate to weigh you down with The Big Question: Should you eat it in front of the TV? Heck, yeah! That just makes it so perfect. My husband also like to put a hint of horseradish on top of his meat loaf. Feel the burn! Just remember that there's a lot of garlic in this dish, so brush your teeth if you're planning on doing any smooching.

911 Moment!

We've all had that nightmare thing happen when we take out our meat loaf, cut into it, and—*yikes!*—it's raw in the center. The quick fix is to just microwave the part that's not cooked (you can also panfry it, too).

Yeah, It's Oy Vey Brisket

I grew up on beef brisket. I'm not talking about those thin slices that you can buy at the deli counter that masquerade as brisket. Oy nay, I say! I mean thick, hot, and tender slices of meat that fall off your fork. (You don't need a knife for this one, honey.) And my grandmother made hers with this dark amber-colored sauce that tasted like sweet onions. Hang on a sec, I think I've just gained five pounds from a memory. . . .

I love brisket because there's no right or wrong way to make it. For example, my mom does an easy, classic thing, which is to smother the meat with Lipton's onion soup mix; but my friend Jack's mom, Sharon, does this cool recipe where she puts stewed tomatoes and Lipton's on top of her brisket. I've tried all the variations, but what I'm gonna give you below is my ultimate favorite. It has garlic mustard and coffee in it, which seems like a strange mix, but it's wonderfully tangy, like a thin barbecue sauce. (Remember to cook this dish on low, because then the flavors really get a chance to blend with each other. The meat will also be extra tender.)

Along with the veggies in the recipe, you can also add those little yellow or red potatoes to the pan—it's one-stop happiness. Believe me, if you do this for company, they're going to freak out. The other night one of my Catholic friends was having his third helping when, between bites, he said, "Wow, Carn! So this is what it's like to be Jewish."

By the way, this is my favorite no-screw-up company entrée, hands down.

Stuff You Need:

One 3-lb. beef brisket

½ cup water

¼ cup dark corn syrup

¼ cup catsup

¼ cup chili sauce

½–1 cup water

¼ cup cider or white-wine vinegar

2 Tbsp. mustard, regular, deli, or garlic flavored

¼ cup Worcestershire sauce

¼ cup oil (vegetable, olive, or whatever's in your pantry)

2 Tbsp. instant-coffee granules

1 tsp. salt

¼ tsp. hot-pepper sauce

1 can stewed tomatoes

1 cup baby carrots

1 onion, quartered

3 celery stalks, cut into 3" pieces

Hit It:

In a medium saucepan over medium-high heat, fire up all the ingredients (except the brisket and veggies) to boiling. Stir or whisk to combine the ingredients, then stir occasionally for 5 minutes. Remove from heat. Now you have your Oy Vey Sauce.

Place the brisket, fat-side up, in a 13" x 9" baking dish or roasting pan. (**Tip:** Just don't pick one that's too big.) Pour the sauce all over the meat, cover the dish with foil, and bake in a 325° oven for 2 hours, basting every half hour with juices.

Add the veggies all around the brisket, mixing the sauce over them. Spread the stewed tomatoes over this and continue to cook, uncovered, for another hour. Continue to baste (hey, all that up and down action must be good for the calves). When ready to serve, remove the meat to a cutting board. Wait 10 minutes and then slice thinly against the grain. Skim the fat from the sauce, then pour the remaining sauce into a bowl or gravy boat.

Serves 6.

Now Serving:

You can add a nice green salad on the side. Of course, mashed potatoes with some of the brisket sauce couldn't hurt.

Carnie Aside-a:

I always recommend using kosher salt, not the table salt you find in those big blue tubes. Kosher salt is sweet and not processed—the bottom line is that it tastes better, and you'll notice the difference.

I Don't Have a Beef with My Mother's Brisket

*This is the easiest brisket recipe around. It's also got more of an onion flavor, which makes it more traditional than my **Yeah, It's Oy Vey Brisket.** By the way, my mom passes this one along from her friend Marci, so "briskets off" to Marci!*

Stuff You Need:

One 5–6 lb. beef brisket

½–¾ jar chili sauce (**Tip:** I like the Homemade brand in the round jar with the white lid, or the kind made by Heinz.)

½–1 can beer (**Tip:** You can use light beer if you'd like.)

½ box brown sugar (**Tip:** You can use ¼ of the package if you like things a little less sweet.)

½–1 whole envelope Lipton's onion soup mix

Hit It:

Put the brisket in a roasting or baking dish, fat-side up. Pour the beer over the meat and spread the chili sauce on top of that; sprinkle on the soup mix and brown sugar. Cover with foil or lid and roast for 5 hours at 325°.

Serves 8.

Carnie Aside-a:

You can freeze this meat a couple of weeks ahead of time before serving, but it's best to cut it into slices before freezing. When you reheat the slices, savor the smell again . . . it's perfect.

Are You Hungry for Hungarian Pork Chops?

To answer that question: Who wouldn't be? It's like asking if you're hungry for your significant other to come up and plant a kiss on you. Are you hungry for a sale at the mall? Are you hungry to win the lottery? How about to have someone come over and make this dish for you?

I guarantee that you have the chops to make this excellent dish. It's the two "c's" in my book: creamy and comforting.

Stuff You Need:

8 wafer-thin cut loin pork chops, bone in

4 Tbsp. butter

½ cup flour

2 Tbsp. sweet Hungarian paprika

1 tsp. salt

1 tsp. pepper

1 tsp. onion powder

½ tsp. dried dill

1 cup sour cream

1 cup chicken broth

1 cup dry white wine

1 large Spanish onion, sliced into rings

1 clove garlic, minced

½ cup sauerkraut, rinsed and drained

1 lb. mushrooms, sliced

1 Tbsp. fresh dill, minced (for garnish)

Hit It:

Mix the flour, salt, pepper, onion powder, dried dill, and 1 Tbsp. of the paprika in a paper bag, then dredge the pork chops through this mixture. (**Huh?** *Dredge* means to lightly pat in a flour mixture or similar to coat, usually before frying or sautéing.) In a large, heavy frying pan, melt 2 tablespoons of the butter; sauté the chops over medium-high heat until lightly browned and crispy, about 2 minutes on each side. (**Tip:** *Do not* crowd the pork chops in the pan—cook 2 batches if necessary, adding more butter if you need to.)

Remove the cooked chops and place them in a large, covered Dutch oven or covered casserole. Don't clean the frying plan; instead, melt the remaining butter in it and sauté the onions and garlic until translucent, then add them to the casserole. Briefly sauté the mushrooms in the pan and add them to the casserole. Add the rest of the butter, sprinkle any remaining seasoned flour in the pan, and stir over medium heat. Pour in the chicken broth and wine, scraping up any bits stuck to the pan; heat and stir until slightly thickened. Add the sauerkraut and the other Tbsp. paprika to the sauce; pour over the ingredients in the casserole. Bake at 350° for an hour or until the chops are tender and falling off the bone. Remove the pork chops with a slotted spatula and place on a deep platter.

Temper the sour cream by mixing the sauce that's left in the pan into it, one tablespoon at a time. (**Huh?** To *temper* something means to slowly drizzle small amounts of a warm preparation into a cooler one while mixing; this way you avoid curdling or cooking heat-sensitive ingredients such as eggs.) Return it to the pan and stir until combined. Sprinkle fresh dill over the warm pork chops, and serve the sauce in a gravy boat on the side.

Serves 4.

Now Serving:

Serve with hot-buttered egg noodles tossed with a tablespoon of poppy seeds or the **Oh-So-Nice Baked Rice** on page 114.

Chili Con Carnie

This recipe is from my good pal Katrina, and it's a beauty. It's good and spicy, plus it's a crowd/spouse-pleaser. Take it to a party, or freeze some in an airtight container and eat it later on when you don't have time to cook. But I don't think it has enough ingredients—ha ha!

Stuff You Need:

2 lbs. ground sirloin, plus 1 lb. lean ground pork (or you can just do 3 lbs. ground sirloin if you want to skip the pork)

1 Tbsp. kosher salt (plus more to taste)

Some freshly ground black pepper

2 Tbsp. ancho chili powder

2 tsp. oregano (preferably Mexican), crushed

2 tsp. thyme

2 Tbsp. olive oil

2 large Spanish onions, chopped

2 large cloves garlic, minced

1 red bell pepper, diced into ½" pieces

1 pasilla chili, diced into ½" pieces

1 can San Marzano diced tomatoes

2 Tbsp. brown sugar

1 Tbsp. ground cumin

1 tsp. Dutch cocoa powder (**Tip:** Use Droste brand or similar. It isn't the same with regular cocoa powder like Hershey's.)

¼ tsp. cinnamon

½ cup mild Anaheim red chili powder

1 dash Worcestershire sauce

5 cups beef or chicken broth

One 12-oz. bottle of beer

2 lbs. frozen or fresh sweet-corn niblets

¼ cup fresh cilantro, chopped finely

2 oz. masa flour, whisked with ½ cup water to make a slurry

(2 Tums [Just take them now—why tempt fate? Mylanta and Pepcid are also good.])

Hit It:

Place the ground meats in a wide bowl. Season with salt and pepper, 1 Tbsp. of the ancho chili powder, and 1 tsp. each of oregano and thyme; mix well with your hands or a spoon and set aside.

In a large Dutch oven, sauté the onions in the olive oil over medium-high heat for 10 minutes, scraping up the browned bits from the bottom of the pan. Add the garlic and sauté for 3 minutes more. Add the meat to the pot and cook on high heat until it's crumbly and browned; add the bell pepper and pasilla chili and sauté for 5 minutes. Stir in the tomatoes, cumin, cocoa, cinnamon, brown sugar, Worcestershire, Anaheim chili powder and the rest of the ancho chili powder, and the rest of the thyme and oregano and cook for 3–4 minutes.

Stir in the broth and beer, breaking it up into bits; reduce the heat and bring to a gentle simmer. Season the chili with salt and pepper to taste; simmer on low, stirring occasionally, for about 45 minutes. Add the corn and chopped cilantro and cook for an additional 15 minutes. Before serving, stir in the masa-flour-and-water mixture and continue cooking until thickened. Correct seasoning with salt and pepper to taste.

Serves 10–12.

Now Serving:

I like to serve this in soup or chili bowls with rice or corn bread and a selection of condiments like sour cream, chopped cilantro, shredded cheddar cheese, and minced fresh onions.

Carnie Aside-a:

This is a fantastic dish to bring to a barbecue or potluck dinner. The good news is that you don't have to be afraid of this chili and the accompanying gas (let's be honest here) because I've skipped the beans. But if you have a sensitive tum, I remind you that Tums are our friend.

Knock on Your Tandoori Barbecued Salmon

This one is quick, different, and simple to make. It's also great for a summertime barbecue.

Stuff You Need:

5 Tbsp. tandoori paste (**Tip:** This is available in the market in the aisle where Indian foods are found, and the best one is Patak's Original.)

1 cup plain low-fat yogurt

2 Tbsp. melted butter

½ a sweet onion, cut into rings

1 whole salmon fillet (about 2 lbs.); or 4 individual fillet pieces, about ½ lb. each—leave the skin on, but be sure to debone

Hit It:

In a small bowl, mix together the tandoori paste and yogurt. Place the salmon, skin-side down, on a platter or Pyrex dish; spread the yogurt mixture evenly on top, coating the fish completely. Cover with plastic wrap and refrigerate for at least 3–4 hours (you can go as long as overnight).

Rub your barbecue's grill with oil before it's turned on or fired up; you can also spray it with Pam. (**Huge Tip:** If you spray Pam *after* you've got the flame going, good-bye eyebrows or house. In other words, don't do it!) When the grill is hot, reduce the temperature to medium; if you're using a charcoal barbecue, wait until the coals are ashy and gray and place the metal rack on the highest notch away from them.

In a large mixing bowl, toss the onion rings in the butter. Using a long-handled spatula, place the salmon, skin-side down, on the grill. Cover the fish with the buttered onion rings and cook (covered) for about 8–12 minutes, depending on the thickness of the fillet(s) and the heat of your grill. Test the salmon for doneness by gently puling apart the fillet at the thickest part to make sure that it's opaque all the way through. Try not to overcook because the fish will continue cooking for a few minutes after it's removed from the heat. Gently lift the salmon from the grill and slide onto a serving platter or some plates.

Serves 4.

Now Serving:

Serve with the **Baja Rice Bake** on page 115 or plain rice pilaf sprinkled with cilantro, plus a cucumber-tomato salad dressed with a light vinaigrette and freshly minced mint leaves. Or serve with **My Big Fat Greek Pasta Salad** on page 36.

Poached Salmon with Unforgetta Bruschetta

"Rob!" I call out.

My other half is in the other room making beautiful music in his studio. "Babe?" I yell. "Sweetie?"

"Huh?" he responds, just like most of the husbands in America.

"Angel, if we have a favorite fish in the world, what would it be?" I ask.

"Nemo," he answers.

"No, no, not an animated fish, although we do love him. What is our favorite fish to eat?" I yell. (It always amazes me that I yell instead of walking down the hall. Why is that?)

"Oh, that salmon thingy you make," he yells back.

Right. Now we have confirmation, everyone. This is my favorite way to cook salmon, and this recipe ensures that you'll have a moist, flavorful, "clean" piece of fish. The way the garlic and cold tomatoes mix together with the hot salmon is magical. And no offense to little Nemo from that Disney movie Rob and I loved, but this is one yummy fish.

This is one of my favorite dishes in the book because it's so light and flavorful.

Stuff You Need:

2 salmon fillets (fresh Atlantic is best), approximately 6 oz. each

Two 14-oz. cans chicken broth

½ cup white wine (optional—you can substitute water if you'd prefer)

1–2 Tbsp. butter

1 Tbsp. balsamic vinegar

Salt and pepper to taste

Hit It:

Prepare the **Bruschetta** (see recipe on the next page) before dealing with the fish. Once you've done so, bring the chicken broth and wine to a boil in a 4-quart saucepan; add the butter. Season the salmon fillets on all sides with salt and pepper, and then pour the balsamic vinegar over both sides as well; gently place them in the boiling liquid. Cover with lid or foil (make sure it's really tight!). After 3 minutes, check for doneness. (**Tip:** To make sure it's done, lift the top of the salmon with a fork—it should be opaque all the way through. Don't let your stove conspire against you. Remember that fish cooks fast, so be careful.)

Carefully remove the fillets from the broth with a slotted spatula and place on a clean paper towel for a moment. Rejoice that you did this so well! Take a sip of a nice beverage . . . wine is optional. Now pat the salmon on top gently with another paper towel. Place the fillets on a platter and cover generously with bruschetta and juices. Prepare to go to heaven!

Serves 2.

General Fish Tip:

How long should you cook your fish? It depends on the method—poaching, grilling, sautéing, or broiling—but remember that fish cooks fast. You're not poisoning people if you take it out sooner rather than later. Just test your piece to make sure that it's flaky and done in the middle (a little bit pink is A-OK). Run your hand over the fish before you cook it to make sure that the bones are out. If you find fine bones, take them out with a pair of tweezers.

(Continued on next page)

Unforgetta Bruschetta

There's nothing like bruschetta. As an appetizer, you can serve it on little toasts; or you can add some sliced red onions, chunks of Italian bread, and fresh pieces of buffalo mozzarella to make a salad. Any way you serve it, bruschetta is gene beyond gene.

Stuff You Need:

6 Roma tomatoes (firm ones are best)

10 large fresh basil leaves

3 large cloves of garlic, finely minced

Juice of ½ of a lemon

¼ cup extra-virgin olive oil

2 Tbsp. good-quality balsamic vinegar

A dash of crushed red pepper

Kosher salt and pepper to taste

Hit It:

Chop the tomatoes and place them in a medium-sized mixing bowl. Chiffonade the basil leaves and add them to the bowl; add all remaining ingredients and stir well. Cover with plastic wrap and set aside until you're ready to serve.

Makes 2 cups.

Now Serving:

Dish this salmon and bruschetta up with mashed potatoes and steamed asparagus.

Carnie Aside-a:

I make this recipe for Rob and me at least once a week because salmon is healthy and heart friendly (omega-3 fatty acids rule!). But prepare yourself for one little fact of life: If you eat this dish, you're going to have major garlic breath!

Just for the Halibut

While I love fish for it's healthy qualities, the truth is that it's not my favorite taste in the world—for example, when I go out to dinner, it's certainly not my top choice. But I can promise you that this recipe makes my mouth water, and it even works for many different fishes.

Stuff You Need:

Four 8-oz. halibut fillets

2 Tbsp. butter

1 shallot, minced

1 Tbsp. capers

2 Tbsp. fresh lemon juice

¼ tsp. fresh lemon zest

¼ cup dry white wine

½ tsp. sea salt

¼ tsp. fresh ground black pepper

1 clove garlic, minced

⅛ cup plus 2 Tbsp. flat-leaf
  Italian parsley, minced

Hit It:

In a large, shallow frying pan, melt the butter on medium-high heat; as soon as it begins to sizzle, add the shallots and garlic and cook for 1–2 minutes, or until the shallots are soft. Lay the halibut fillets in the pan and sauté for about 2 minutes; turn them over and sauté for about 2 more minutes. Add the wine and all other ingredients over the fillets; cover and continue to cook for an additional minute or so, until the fillets flake easily and are opaque all the way through. Remove the fish from the pan. Use a large spoon to collect the pan juices and capers; drizzle over the fillets and then sprinkle with the remaining 2 Tbsp. parsley.

Serves 4.

Now Serving:

Dish up with any kind of rice, mashed potatoes, or steamed asparagus.

Tuna Canoodle

Here's a recipe from my good friend Owen, and I think that it's definitely her best. Everyone will rave. In fact, let's call her and ask her about it. . . .

Me: Hi, Owen. I'm putting one of your recipes in the book.

Owen: Oh God! But I'm honored.

Me: Can you fax over the recipe?

Owen: Um, do you care that it starts with a mix?

Me: No. I want it exactly as you make it.

Owen: Okay, get that Kraft Deluxe Mac and Cheese, the one with the foil packet. [Loud crashes in the background.] Just a second, Carn. . . . Honey, I'm on the phone—Mommy is making something with Aunt Carnie. [Moments pass. I roast an entire turkey in the meantime—or so it seems.]

Me: Owen . . . Owen? . . . Are you there? Are you alive?

Owen: I gotta go be a mom, Carn. I'll call you back in two minutes.

Me: Oh God. Never mind. Just fax it to me.

Gotta love Owen. Her kids always come first.

Stuff You Need:

1 box Kraft Deluxe Mac and Cheese

2 Tbsp. butter

½ cup celery, chopped

½ cup onion, chopped

One 6-oz. can white albacore
   tuna packed in water

1 pkg. (2 cups) shredded cheddar cheese

1 cup bread crumbs

1 cup milk

½ cup sour cream

1 Tbsp. fresh or dried dill

1 tomato, sliced

Hit It:

Preheat oven to 375°. Heat the butter in a pan and sauté the onion and celery in it until soft. Add the tuna and sauté until warm; set aside.

Boil water for the noodles that come in the mac-and-cheese mix. Place the foil cheese packet in so that the cheese softens, but don't open the packet or it will be quite the boiling mess. (Be careful when you take the packet out of the water because it will be hot.) Cook and drain the pasta in the package, mix in the cheese packet, and blend well. Add the milk and sour cream, along with half the shredded-cheese package. (Save the other half for the top of the casserole.)

Add the tuna mix to the mac and cheese; pour the entire mixture into a casserole pan and smooth the top flat with spatula. Dust the top lightly with bread crumbs. Add a layer of tomatoes and finish with the rest of the cheese. Bake for 25 minutes or until you see the edges bubble. Take the dish out of the oven (mmm, it smells yummy) and let it sit for 15 minutes before serving. Hug your child—Owen would want you to!

Serves 8.

Now Serving:

I love to eat this dish with a simple green salad and the **Berry, Berry Delicious Bars** on page 138 for dessert. Okay, I know you're thumbing your way there now, thinking, *Did someone say dessert?* It's okay—that's what I'd do, too.

Mock Cannelloni for My "Hony"

There's a bit of prep here, around 45 minutes to an hour, but it's so worth it. What a wonderful dish to serve at a dinner party or to some very hungry men. Serve with extra sauce and a nice glass of Zinfandel or Pinot Grigio.

P.S. The title is not a typo. I don't always call Rob "my honey"—I prefer to call him "my hoe-nee." It just sounds sweeter.

Stuff You Need:

1 appetite—this isn't the dish to eat after downing a pizza

1 Tbsp. olive oil

1 lb. ground turkey breast

½ lb. mortadella, roughly minced (**Huh?** Mortadella is a type of smoked Italian sausage that you can generally find at a deli)

One 10-oz. pkg. frozen spinach, chopped (thawed and drained or squeezed dry); or 10 oz. fresh spinach

½ Spanish onion, minced finely

1 large garlic clove, minced

1 cup fresh mushrooms, minced

1 Tbsp. fresh oregano, minced

2 tsp. fresh basil, minced

1 Tbsp. fresh Italian flat-leaf parsley, minced

1 tsp. salt

½ tsp. pepper

¼ cup dry bread crumbs, plain

2 eggs, beaten

2 oz. Parmesan cheese, shredded

2 oz. Havarti cheese, grated

12 square egg-roll wrappers (I like Dynasty's brand)

For the Sauce

(note that this recipe is doubled so you have some for the side):

½ cup butter

½ cup flour

2 cups chicken broth

2 cups half-and-half

½ tsp. Dijon mustard

½ tsp. ground nutmeg

Salt and pepper to taste

Hit It:

Preheat oven to 375°. Heat the olive oil in a heavy frying pan; add the onions and sauté until translucent. Add the ground turkey and sauté until no longer pink, breaking up the large lumps with the back of a wooden spoon. Add the garlic, mortadella, spinach, mushrooms, parsley, basil, oregano, pepper, and salt; sauté on medium heat for 3 minutes. Remove from heat and mix in the bread crumbs, cheeses, and eggs. While the mixture is cooling, make the sauce.

In a small saucepan, melt the butter over medium heat. Stir in the flour and cook until bubbly, but not browned; add the broth and stir. Add the half-and-half, Dijon mustard, and nutmeg one at a time—be sure to stir after each has been added. Cook, stirring until thickened; salt and pepper to taste. (**Tip:** Remember that the cannelloni is already seasoned.)

(Continued on next page)

Lightly grease a 13" x 9" baking pan. Take the cooled turkey mixture and spoon ⅟₁₂ of it across the center of an egg-roll wrapper. Fold the top part over the filling, turn in the right side toward the middle and do the same with the left side, and roll the top part down and over like you're making a burrito. Gently place, seam-side down, in the pan. Repeat with the remaining 11 cannelloni. (Isn't it fun? Have your kids jump in and help.) Pour half of the sauce over the cannelloni and reserve half to serve on the side. Sprinkle with the remaining Parmesan and bake until bubbling and the top is lightly browned.

Serves 8.

Now Serving:

This is a very filling dish, so I usually avoid any serious sides other than a few steamed veggies or a simple green salad with the **Raspberry Dressing** on page 31. This is also a dish where you'll want to make sure that there's a padlock on the fridge, because it's divine served cold the next day.

Miso Hungry

My dear friend Kim Goodwin's mom, Miko, is Japanese, and this is her authentic miso soup (otherwise known as Okinawa Soup). She says that it's actually more than just a meal: "It soothes your soul and warms your heart."

Thank you, Miko Yeyonahara. Kon-bon-wa. (Translation: "I love you.")

Stuff You Need:

6 cups water

½ cup miso
(brown soybean paste)

½ bag of spinach
(approximately 6 oz.) washed
thoroughly and roughly chopped

1 pack somen noodles
(**Tip:** Just use one portion
of the four sections of noodles.)

2 scallions with white parts,
thinly sliced

Salt to taste

1 cup tofu, cubed (optional)

Hit It:

In a large pot, bring 3 cups of the water to a boil; place the Somen noodles in and bring to a second boil. Drain the noodles, then massage and rinse them with your hands (**Tip:** I know this sounds weird, but do it! It helps get rid of the starch.) When the noodles make a squeaky noise, the starch is out.

Bring the remaining 3 cups of water to a boil; add the miso and bring to a second boil. Add the spinach and bring to another boil; then shut off the heat and add the scallions, seasoning with salt. Add the noodles (and the tofu, if you like).

Serves 4–6.

Now Serving:

Place in a large bowl and serve family style. Add your favorite salad on the side, along with a cup of fresh white rice per person.

Lasagna with Mini-Me Balls

It's Saturday night and my friends Tiffany and Cindy are over. We're sitting around watching <u>Entertainment Tonight</u> and getting the latest juice on our favorite stars. We figure that maybe we'll be starving soon—after all, all that celeb news would make anyone hungry. It's definitely time for some delish lasagna.

A quick trip to the store later and we're regrouping in the kitchen. Everybody has a job: I mix the meat, Tiff blanches the veggies, Cindy beats the eggs. It's not like we don't trust her with bigger jobs, but . . . oh, in between we read aloud the six magazines we bought at the store. In other words, it's the perfect Saturday night with nothing much to do.

When Rob comes out of the studio, he says the magic words: "What smells so good?"

I look at him and say, "You're good-lookin'."

He hugs me and says, "You're good-lookin' <u>and</u> good-cookin'."

No wonder why I slave over a hot stove for my guy.

Stuff You Need:

½ lb. lean ground beef

½ cup fresh bread crumbs (**Tip:** Fresh slices of white bread in a mini food processor make perfect bread crumbs. Try it—it will add lovely flavor and moisture to your foods.)

1 tsp. fresh parsley, minced

1 egg, lightly beaten

1 pkg. lasagna noodles (about ¾ lb.); you can also use the oven-ready kind— Barilla makes some great ones

3 Tbsp. olive oil

½ tsp. salt

⅛ tsp. pepper

4 cups prepared meat sauce (I like Ragú. Call me "low maintenance" . . . just don't tell anybody)

½ lb. Italian sweet sausage, casing removed (sauté the meat until brown and crumbly)

2 hard-boiled eggs, thinly sliced

¾ lb. (or 12 oz.) mozzarella cheese, freshly grated

½ cup Parmesan cheese, freshly shredded or grated

For the Ricotta Filling:

1 lb. whole-milk ricotta cheese

¼ tsp. nutmeg

2 Tbsp. finely chopped flat-leaf parsley

1 egg, lightly beaten

½ tsp. salt

Hit It:

Mix together the ground beef and bread crumbs in a medium-size bowl with 1 beaten egg, pepper, and ½ tsp. salt. Make meatballs the size of a large pearl onion (we're talking approximately 1½" in diameter). Fry in 2 Tbsp. of the olive oil until browned; drain and set aside.

Blanch the noodles. (**Huh?** *Blanching* means that you make the noodle water boil and then put each strip of lasagna in it for about a minute. The noodles will become a little bit tender on each side, but won't even come close to cooking through.) Take them out of the water with tongs so that you don't burn yourself, then lay the noodles out on a paper towel to absorb the extra water. While baking, the noodles will also absorb water from the other ingredients and become the perfect, not-at-all-mushy, no-way-gushy, noodles. It's gene. (Or you can save yourself all this trouble and use already-baked noodles. That's what I do.) Now the noodles are ready for the lasagna pan.

Prepare the ricotta filling (while doing so, imagine that you're Carmela Soprano). In a medium bowl, combine the ricotta cheese, nutmeg, and parsley with the remaining ½ tsp. salt and the other beaten egg; mix with a wooden spoon. Take a breath—you've done a lot so far.

Preheat the oven to 375° and don't eat the raw-ricotta mix out of the bowl. (That would be gross, although it smells so great.) Rub a 13" x 9" baking pan with the remaining olive oil and use a ladle to spoon some meat sauce on top. Place a layer of cooked lasagna noodles over this, overlapping slightly to cover the bottom of the pan. Drop the ricotta filling by the spoonful on top of the noodles;

smooth with the back of the spoon or spread it out with your freshly washed fingers. Scatter a layer of meatballs over the ricotta, followed by half of the sausage, and then sprinkle half of the sliced boiled eggs on top of that delicious deal. Top with half of the mozzarella and Parmesan. Repeat layers, ending with a layer of noodles, top with the remaining sauce, and finish with the remaining cheese.

Bake covered for 45 minutes until golden brown; uncover and bake for an additional 15 minutes. (**Tip:** Try to clean up the kitchen now—believe me, you'll hug yourself later.) Remove from the oven and let rest for 10 minutes before serving. Add fresh chopped parsley on top for garnish. Yes, it does look pretty! Gaze at the pan in awe as you marvel, *I actually made this thing!*

Serves 10.

Now Serving:

This is a very filling meal (in fact, don't wear your new Levi's with this one). I tend to fill up on the meatballs and eat my way around the noodles, which is also good if you're into skipping carbs. By the way, I like to serve this dish with a simple green salad filled with fresh cucumbers, carrots, mushrooms, and tomatoes, with a little light vinaigrette splashed over it.

If you feel adventurous when it comes to calories, add some doughy Italian bread. And if you want to throw all caution to the wind, spread some butter, dried herbs (like basil and oregano), fresh minced garlic, and kosher salt on it to make garlic bread. Prepare to spend the rest of the night sacked out on the couch after this meal. It might be an effort to even reach for the remote.

Carnie Aside-a:

If I don't have time to make a lasagna, I might just make the meatballs, which is also what turns this dish into The Skinny. If you're on a low-carb diet, then just eat meatballs for dinner covered with some delicious sauce (either homemade or in a jar). But if you're feeling a little carb hungry, then boil up some of your favorite pasta to serve on the side or under those meatballs.

The Music That Makes Me Cook

Honestly, it helps me in the kitchen if I grab a CD and blast any of the following on my stereo:

"Respect" by Aretha Franklin
"September" by Earth Wind & Fire
"Rock Lobster" by the B-52's
Anything by Donna Summer
"Take It Easy" or "Already Gone" by the Eagles
"Working Day and Night" (or any song) by Michael Jackson
"Barracuda" by Heart
"Stayin' Alive" by the Bee Gees
Anything by Sade
Any big band or swing, especially if it's done by Ella Fitzgerald
"Fun, Fun, Fun" by The Beach Boys (Oh, come on—you've gotta give me one!)

Ain't Too Proud to Veg Lasagna
(with Mushroom Béchamel)

*I must say it right now: This is the best recipe in the entire book (besides, of course, the **Fall to Your Knees Mac and Cheese** on page 117). It's so good that when someone eats a bite, they have a tendency to close their eyes while chewing. I know, I know—it's hard to eat with your eyes closed, but sometimes you must allow it (unless the guest starts spilling food all over the table).*

The good news is that there are only 6 noodles per dish. And I've decided to make this with no-boil noodles because it turns out the best that way.

Another word of warning: It tastes great the next day . . . that is, if it makes it to the next day.

Stuff You Need:

One 8-oz. pkg. no-boil lasagna noodles
(**Tip:** You're only going to use 6.)

3 Tbsp. unsalted butter

2 large garlic cloves, minced

¼ cup flour

2 cups milk

2 cups cream

1 tsp. salt

¼ tsp. nutmeg

⅛ tsp. cayenne pepper

2½ cups mozzarella cheese, grated
(divide into 1 cup and 1½ cups)

1½ cups fresh Parmesan Reggiano
cheese, shredded

4 oz. cream cheese (the original
firm variety, not in the tub), sliced

½ tsp. sweet paprika

1½ cups broccoli florets
(precook by microwaving with
2 Tbsp. water in a Ziploc bag for
3 minutes, or steaming until
firm yet tender)

1 cup carrots, shredded (precook
the same as the broccoli above)

1 cup zucchini, sliced or julienned (precook the same as the broccoli above)

1 lb. mushrooms, sliced and briefly
sautéed in 1 Tbsp. butter
(reserve the juice)

1 cup fresh or frozen corn kernels,
thawed and drained

Your good china. This dish is worth it.

Hit It:

Preheat oven to 325°. Spray a 13" x 9" casserole dish with a nonstick cooking spray. In a medium saucepan, combine the butter and garlic and cook over moderate heat for 1 minute—don't let it brown. Add flour and cook, stirring for 1–2 minutes (**Tip:** We're making what's called a *roux*, which is the base of the sauce and what makes it thick.) While whisking constantly, slowly drizzle in 1 cup each of the milk and cream; continue whisking at a simmer until thickened. Add the remaining milk and cream, along with the cream cheese (which should be sliced into bits), salt, pepper, nutmeg, and cayenne; stir frequently.

Reduce heat to low and continue to simmer, stirring frequently for 5 minutes. Remove the sauce from heat. Combine 1 cup of the Parmesan with 1 cup of the mozzarella; add to the sauce and stir until cheeses are melted. Add sautéed mushrooms and their reserved juices, stirring gently to combine.

Spread a thin layer of sauce on the bottom of the casserole dish. Place 3 lasagna noodles with a little sauce in between them in the dish; sprinkle half of the prepared vegetables over that. Ladle half of the sauce over the vegetables, along with 1 cup mozzarella. Add the 3 other noodles. Repeat layers, ending with sauce. Top with remaining mozzarella, Parmesan, and paprika; cover with foil. Bake for 50–55 minutes or until bubbling, golden brown, and hot. Remove foil, turn the oven up to 350° and bake for 10 more minutes uncovered. Let stand for 15 minutes before shoving it into your mouth because that's *honestly* what you'll want to do.

Serves 8.

Now Serving:

This dish is perfect with your favorite dinner salad and **Everybody Was Tofu Biting** (page 153) or **Guilt-Free Let It Snow Cones** (page 157).

And Now Meet My Meat Sauce
(with Spaghetti, of Course)

There are so many varieties of meat sauce out there that are delicious, but this one is a quick and easy surprise that has a secret: It features double the meat. I made up this recipe after years of experimenting, and let me say one thing right off the bat: I have no shame that one of the ingredients is sauce from a jar. You're still making this baby from scratch—and when your own mother doesn't believe that you made it, then you know you're doing good things in the kitchen.

In fact, my mom was eating this just the other day when she looked at her son-in-law in disbelief. "Rob, are you kidding me?" she said. "How do you live with her cooking like this? I'd be eating all day long."

Rob replied: "I know! I know! I'm on a diet . . . but could you please pass the sauce?"

Stuff You Need:

1 lb. spaghetti

1 lb. ground sirloin

1 jar of a high-quality meat sauce—
   spend a few dollars on the really
   good stuff

One 28-oz. can whole Roma tomatoes,
   roughly chopped or quartered (San
   Marzano is my pick)

½ can (3 oz.) tomato paste

½ cup good-quality red wine (optional)

½ cup each carrots, celery, and
   onions, finely chopped

3 garlic cloves, minced

½ tsp. each dried basil, dried
   parsley, Italian seasoning, and
   garlic powder

1 bay leaf

Salt and pepper to taste

½ tsp. red pepper flakes

½ tsp. dried oregano

¼ cup heavy whipping cream

1 tsp. sugar

4 Tbsp. butter, divided in half

2 Tbsp. plus ¼ cup olive oil

Fresh parsley for garnish

Parmesan cheese

Hit It:

In a nonstick skillet, brown the ground beef; add the basil, parsley, Italian seasoning, garlic power, salt, and pepper. In a separate large pot, heat 2 Tbsp. of the olive oil and 2 Tbsp. of the butter; add the carrots, celery, and onions, and cook until soft. This should take 3–5 minutes. Add the garlic and cook for another minute. (**Tip:** You never want to add garlic too early because you don't want it to brown and taste bitter.) Add a little salt and pepper; pour in the meat sauce and stir to combine.

Meanwhile, boil water in a large pot for your pasta, adding a little olive oil and salt to it. Get back to your sauce and add the bay leaf, wine (if you want), and Roma tomatoes, including the juice. Add the tomato paste and stir until well incorporated; stir in the cooked beef, and simmer on a low to medium flame. (**Tip:** If you hear crazy popping sounds from your sauce, turn the heat down a little bit. This way you won't burn your sauce on the bottom of the pan.) Toss in the red pepper flakes, sugar, cream, and oregano; let simmer for 20–25 minutes. Add the remaining olive oil and butter, and stir well.

Serves 8.

Now Serving:

Pour all the sauce over the cooked noodles and toss to combine. It's the perfect amount of sauce for a 1-lb. box of noodles. Garnish with fresh parsley and Parmesan cheese, and serve with garlic bread (if you dare). Watch your own mother go back for seconds.

CHAPTER SIX

Side Dishes— You Won't Want to Push These Aside

Who would the Lone Ranger be without Tonto? Fred without Barney? Mary without Rhoda? Carrie without Samantha, Charlotte, and Miranda? Everyone needs a good sidekick . . . and this includes your favorite entrees. I have to admit that even if the entrée is wonderful, it's the sides that have me excited and racing to the dinner table!

Righteous Mashed Potatoes with Roasted Garlic:
THE SINFUL

One day my friend Tiffany and I came home from the fourth grade extremely bored and sort of hungry. I don't remember who had the crazy idea of whipping up a product that's so easy to find that it's even available at the gas station . . . but I think it might have been me.

"I know!" I said. "Let's make potato chips!"

Tiff was game, and agreed to haul my mother's 10-pound bag of taters out of the closet with me. After locating the two biggest knives known to the human race, we began to cut huge wedges of potatoes—little did we know that you're supposed to slice potato chips super thin. (I guess we thought they'd lose something in the baking.)

Anyway, we lined up our potato hunks on a metal pan and forgot to spray the bottom. Not only did these potato blobs never really get soft, but the bottoms of them were so burned onto the pan that there was only one solution: Yes, we ate what we could salvage of the "chips" (and I use that word loosely). Then we promptly found the largest garbage bags possible and threw everything out—including the pan—before my mom got home.

These days Tiffany and I don't eat potato chips—instead, we get our taters in other, far-yummier forms. We're older. We're wiser. And the potatoes are more cooperative, too, which is good news for everyone, including the local fire department.

Stuff You Need:

2½ lbs. potatoes (Yukon gold or Idaho russet are good), cut into 1" slices

1 stick (8 oz.—I know . . . calm down!) butter, melted

4 oz. cream cheese (at room temp.)

4 oz. sour cream

¼ cup heavy whipping cream, warmed

¼ cup half-and-half or milk

1 tsp. salt (more to taste)

Pepper to taste

Hit It:

Place the potatoes in a large, tall saucepan, covering with at least 1–2" cold water. Add the salt and bring to a boil. Cover with foil partway, and reduce the heat to medium, cooking potatoes until they're tender when pierced with a fork (this usually takes about 15–20 minutes). Using a colander, drain the potatoes and then return them to the pan.

Heat and stir around the potatoes until the liquid has evaporated. Mash the potatoes by hand with a potato masher until very smooth and the lumps are virtually gone (although I actually prefer them lumpy). Add the butter in a slow pour while beating constantly. Add the cream cheese (in little pieces), the sour cream, the heated cream, and the half-and-half, while stirring constantly.

Place the **Roasted Garlic** in (see next page) and blend well. Salt and pepper to taste.

Serves 8.

Roasted Garlic

Stuff You Need:

1 head garlic

2 Tbsp. olive oil

Salt and pepper to taste

Hit It:

Preheat oven to 400°. Cut the top off the pointy side of the garlic head with a sharp knife (so you see the cloves exposed). Set the garlic on a piece of foil, approximately 8" on all sides; drizzle the olive oil over the top, and sprinkle with some salt and pepper to taste. Bring all sides of the foil up together tightly, making a pouch for the garlic. Roast in the oven for about 45 minutes, until the cloves are tender and mushy—they should be easy to squeeze out. You won't believe the aroma in your home while the garlic is cooking—it's probably my favorite smell on Earth. . . .

Carefully unwrap the garlic and let it cool. When it's cool enough to handle, squeeze the cloves (God's gift to man!) into a bowl. (**Tip:** Remember to discard the shells.) Mash it with a fork until it becomes a heavenly paste; add this to the potatoes and let the magic begin! Seriously, folks, it doesn't get any better than this. (In fact, my alternate name for this recipe is **The Best Thing Ever!**)

An Amazing Variation:

Add ½ cup already sautéed, caramelized onions to the mashed potatoes. All you need to do is slice up a big onion into ringlets and let it cook in a skillet in about half a stick of butter on low heat. Stir occasionally until brown. Oh my Lordy, Lordy!

Now Serving:

Ohh, baby. These potatoes are the real deal. Eat them with just about anything.

Righteous Roasted Mashed Potatoes with Roasted Garlic:
THE SKINNY

Substitute 4 oz. of I Can't Believe It's Not Butter for the stick of butter, use fat-free cream cheese and sour cream, and substitute ½ cup low-sodium chicken broth for the heavy whipping cream. Use some Lawry's Seasoned Salt plus pepper to taste. The cooking directions are the same.

More Skinny Potatoes:

Mix together ¼ cup olive oil, 1 tsp. kosher salt, and 1 Tbsp. fresh rosemary, a very powerful herb; mash with the garlic and add to the potatoes. The flavor you create here will mask what you're missing. (**Tip:** Add a hint of nutmeg for an extra blast of flavor.)

Carnie Aside-a:

These days, I've learned to have a large tablespoon's worth of mashed potatoes as my portion and make my protein the priority at a meal. But it's not easy—after all, I used to fill half a plate with potatoes! Anyway, just savor what you can eat.

Adding homemade roasted garlic sends me to another planet. If that isn't good enough for you, add a tablespoon of chopped fresh chives and go to another *galaxy*.

Daniel's White-Trash Potatoes
(I Think Not)

My friend Daniel is perfect at doing everything: His house is perfect; and he's the perfect makeup artist, hairdresser, and friend. Oh, and adding to his long list of talents is the fact that the guy makes the perfect potatoes. Who'd a thunk it? Actually, Daniel's a great cook, and he was kind enough to let me borrow this recipe. It's the main event at any dinner. (The secret is the meat that's in the potatoes.) By the way, these are just about the best potatoes I've ever eaten.

A few notes: This is a dish that takes some prep, but it's worth it. And it's not a dish for gastric-bypass patients because it's so rich. Just take one or two bites if you must. I understand, though . . . they're hard to resist.

Stuff You Need:

10–12 white potatoes, about the size of a lemon, peeled and sliced ⅛" wide (store in a bowl of water to keep from browning)

¼ cup pancetta (thick cut—use the meat part only, not the fat) or prosciutto

¼ cup bacon (thick cut—use the meat part only, not the fat)

¼ cup Italian salami

¾ stick butter, cut into tiny cubes

2 Tbsp. olive oil

2 cups half-and-half (divided evenly)

½ cup whipping cream

¼ cup sour cream

¼ cup cream cheese

3 cloves garlic, placed through a press (or very finely chopped)

8 shallots, finely chopped

½ cup whole-milk mozzarella cheese, shredded

½ cup Gruyère cheese, shredded

1½ cups sharp white cheddar cheese, shredded

½ cup provolone cheese, grated

¼ cup mizithra cheese, shredded
(**Huh?** Mizithra is a dried type of ricotta with a very unique flavor that's heavenly, but it's hard to find—so it's optional here.)

2 heaping tsp. parsley, chopped
(**Tip:** Save a little more for garnish.)

Hit It:

Fry the bacon and pancetta in a small nonstick skillet until chewy and slightly crispy (but not burnt!); set aside. In a medium mixing bowl, combine 1 cup of the half-and-half with the whipping cream, sour cream, cream cheese, and garlic. Puree with a hand blender until the cream cheese is broken up and it's pureed a bit (if you don't have a hand blender, then use a regular blender or food processor); set aside. Combine the mozzarella, Gruyère, sharp white cheddar, provolone, Parmesan, and mizithra cheeses in a bowl; set aside. Set oven to 375°.

Drizzle a 13" x 9" baking dish with the olive oil and scatter ⅓ of the butter cubes all around. Start your layering process: Put one layer of potatoes in rows that overlap each other slightly. Scatter half of the cooked meats and salami all around, and then pour half of the cream mixture on top. Sprinkle 1 Tbsp. of the parsley and 1 tsp. of the shallots, plus a few nice handfuls of the cheeses, over that. (Are you ready for this? Okay, moving on. . . .) Repeat the layers.

Pour the reserved ½ cup of half-and-half over the top and then spoon the shallots in a strip across the middle (they'll caramelize beautifully when it bakes); scatter a few dots of butter right on top. Bake for approximately 30–45 minutes, watching carefully toward the end—you want it a nice golden brown color and bubbling. Garnish with a little parsley, and let it cool for a few minutes before serving. Don't pass out after you taste it. It's that good.

Serves 8–10.

Carnie Aside-a:

As an alternative, you could use just one layer of the cooked meats and salami inside the potatoes and then spoon the rest on either side of the shallots on the top. This looks really pretty with some fresh parsley, too. It's totally decadent!

My Sweet Mom's Sweet Potatoes

There comes a point in every woman's life when she finally realizes that she's hot. For me, I knew I was sizzling on Thanksgiving morning, 1999. It was a feeling so strong that it was undeniable and unforgettable. . . .

I was a little nervous because it was my first time making a major meal for the fam, so I was dreaming stuffing, tossing and turning over giblets, and moaning things in my sleep about what I wanted to do with cranberry sauce.

*At 4 A.M., I padded into the chilly kitchen in my huge blue-flannel nightgown with the romantic, poofy princess sleeves, and got out my bread crumbs. Sadly for them, I didn't soak them—instead, I drowned them in water. I mean, it was like they were on the <u>Titanic</u> in my kitchen. (**Tip:** It's not good if you use fresh bread for stuffing; stale bread soaks up the moisture.)*

Ignoring that mess, I cranked the knob on my Kenmore stove, and I gingerly placed the cut-up veggies for the stuffing in the pan while thinking, <u>Oh man, it's sort of hot in here. Maybe I should turn on the air-conditioning.</u> I didn't leave the stove, and as the minutes passed, my face was flushed and this strange warmth seemed to creep up my spine.

The truth was that I was flambéing what I now like to call "the <u>real</u> 'other white meat.'" That would be me.

"Oh my God!" I screamed, after I noticed that my nightgown sleeve wasn't blue anymore, but bright orange. It was burning fast, but luckily the flame hadn't exactly hit my skin. I'm not certain about fire-safety tips, but I'm pretty sure the local fire department wouldn't sanction what I did in this emergency: I basically ran around the kitchen while crying for God at the top of my lungs—and forget a fire extinguisher, I was banging my arm with my cool, not-on-fire hand.

When the crisis was over, I sat down at my kitchen table, but I couldn't even drink any coffee because my hands were shaking so bad. "You're lucky. Calm down," I told myself. But I immediately phoned my mother, waking her out of a sound sleep.

"Good morning, Mom. Happy Thanksgiving, and I just set myself on fire," I blurted out.

"What?!" she yelled.

In the spirit of the holiday season, here's another recipe that leaves me warm all over. It's Mom's specialty.

Stuff You Need:

3 cans (17 oz. each) whole sweet potatoes, drained (sometimes I add a few more potatoes)

1 can (21 oz.) apple-pie filling

1 can (21 oz.) cherry-pie filling

2 Tbsp. butter or margarine, cut in small pieces

1 tsp. cinnamon

1 Tbsp. brown sugar

A bag of small marshmallows

Dried apricots, prunes, and raisins to taste

Maple syrup

Hit It:

Preheat oven to 350°. In a greased baking dish, layer the sweet potatoes with the apple- and cherry-pie filling. Dot with butter, sprinkle with cinnamon, add the dried fruits and marshmallows, and sprinkle brown sugar over the entire mixture. Begin to layer the heck out of this dish by repeating the above.

Bake for about an hour or until the marshmallows melt or bubble. (**Tip:** If you see this burning, cover with tinfoil during baking; if you see *yourself* burning, call 911.)

Serves 10.

Carnie's Roasted Baby Taters

Stuff You Need:

1 pkg. baby Yukon gold potatoes,
    about 1 lb. (12–15 baby potatoes)

Olive oil (**Tip:** I use extra virgin.)

¼ tsp. garlic powder

¼ tsp. onion powder

A pinch of cayenne pepper

½ tsp. kosher salt

1 Tbsp. fresh chives, finely chopped

1 tsp. fresh parsley, finely chopped

Hit It:

Preheat oven to 400°. Cut the potatoes in half and place them in a 8" x 8" Pyrex dish. Generously sprinkle the potatoes with olive oil and toss to coat, using your hands. Sprinkle the garlic powder, onion powder, cayenne pepper, and kosher salt on top; toss again to coat evenly.

Bake for 30 minutes, checking the potatoes occasionally and moving them around to prevent sticking. The taters are ready when the outside is golden brown and they're tender when pierced with a fork. Transfer into a serving bowl, making sure that you scrape all the yummy bits off the bottom of the pan. Garnish with fresh chives and parsley.

Serves 4–6.

Carnie Aside-a:

What else is for dinner? Who cares? I don't!

Oh-So-Nice Baked Rice

It's great to make a recipe that's complicated and unique, but there are other times when it's really comforting to just get down to basics.

This is one of my favorite easy, comforting sides for a cold winter day. This is inspired by The Fannie Farmer Cookbook. What can I say? I'm a big fan!

Stuff You Need:

⅓ cup onion, finely chopped

2 Tbsp. butter

1 cup rice

2 cups chicken broth

1 tsp. dried basil

½ tsp. dried oregano

⅛ cup fresh parsley, minced

Salt and pepper to taste

Hit It:

Preheat the oven to 375°. Sauté the onion in the butter for 3 minutes; add the rice and stir for 2–3 minutes. Add the broth, oregano, and basil and mix well. Transfer to a 1½ quart casserole; cover and bake for 30 minutes. Remove from the oven and let rest for 5 minutes, uncovered. Stir in the parsley and serve.

Serves 6–8.

Now Serving:

This is a great side with **Perfect Breasts and Thighs** (page 84) or **Just for the Halibut** (page 98). I also love it with **Give Your Company the Bird** (page 83) or **Chicken Cacciatore If You Can** (page 81). It also tastes delish with **Poached Salmon with Unforgetta Bruschetta** (page 97).

Baja Rice Bake

Stuff You Need:

2 cups chicken broth

¾ cup white rice (**Important Tip:** These measurements are for converted rice, such as Uncle Ben's. If you use a long-grain rice such as basmati, substitute 1 cup rice and 1¾ cups broth.)

2 cups sour cream

2 cloves garlic, finely minced

One 8-oz. can diced green chilis

½ cup scallions (with some tops), sliced

1 tsp. oregano

½ tsp. salt

¼ tsp. black pepper

¼ cup Italian flat-leaf parsley, minced

3 zucchini, ends trimmed, sliced into ¼" coins

3 Roma tomatoes, chopped and drained

2 cups Monterey jack cheese, grated

2 cups cotija cheese, grated, or mild feta cheese, crumbled

Hit It:

In a large saucepan, bring the broth to a boil and add the rice; reduce to a simmer. Cover and cook for 20 minutes or until the liquid is absorbed and the rice is tender. Mix together the next 8 ingredients in a bowl. Lightly grease a 4- or 5-quart casserole and layer ½ the rice, ½ the sour-cream mixture, ½ the zucchini, ½ the tomatoes, and ½ the cheeses; repeat the layers, topping the whole thing with cheese. Bake in a 350° oven for 50 minutes, and let stand 10 minutes before serving. Mmm!

Serves 8–10.

Grandma Mae's Cheese Soufflé

This is a dish that I used to beg my grandmother over and over again to make for me. She made it the best, but this is pretty darn close. I know she'd be proud.

Stuff You Need:

1 whole loaf egg bread (remove the crusts and cube into 1" pieces)

1 lb. (16 oz.) sharp cheddar cheese, finely grated

10 eggs

1 qt. milk

½–⅓ stick margarine

½ tsp. salt

Hit It:

Grease a 13" x 9" Pyrex dish. Evenly spread half of the bread with half the margarine. (**Tip:** Dot it on.) Sprinkle half of the portion of grated cheese; repeat for the second layer. Beat 10 eggs very, very, well and then add the salt to them. (Say "oy vey" while doing it for Mae.)

Slowly spread the egg mixture over the entire top; pour a whole quart of milk over this. Bake at 325° (unless you're using a metal pan; in which case, bake at 350°) for 75 minutes, until the crust is golden brown. If it starts to brown too early, put a loose piece of foil on top. (**Hint:** Don't eat it while it's too hot or you'll burn your tongue. But what price pain?)

Serves 10.

Fall to Your Knees Mac and Cheese

And now for my favorite thing on Planet Earth: that would be mac and cheese. There is <u>nothing</u> I love more, and honestly, I could eat this all day long. (It's partially what made me fat.) It's what I always wish I could have more of now. And speaking of wanting more, this version of mac and cheese has more cheese than noodles. What could be better? It's what I dream about at night. Call me crazy Carnie.

Mac and cheese is the ultimate comfort food and the best crowd-pleaser I know. It takes you backward, forward, sideways, and up and down, and makes you do that little "happy dance" you do inside when something really hits the spot . . . until you step on the scale, that is. This dish has more cheese than noodles . . . what could be better? ☺

For a split second, I thought about offering you a skinnier version of the mac, but let's get real. Just have the real thing and eat less. You could also do an extra 45 minutes on the treadmill. It's sooo worth it.

Stuff You Need:

3½ cups large elbow macaroni

12 oz. Velveeta cheese, cut into 1" squares

10 oz. white Vermont cheddar cheese, cut into 1" squares

15 oz. Gruyère cheese, shredded

1–2 cups of jack and cheddar cheese (combined), shredded

4 oz. cream cheese (at room temp.)

⅔ cup sour cream

1⅓ cups heavy cream

1⅓ cups half-and-half

1 egg

2⅔ Tbsp. flour

1 Tbsp. Worcestershire sauce

1 tsp. garlic powder

1 tsp. onion powder

1 tsp. dry mustard powder

⅛–¼ tsp. cayenne pepper

⅛ tsp. nutmeg (fresh if you have it)

1 tsp. kosher salt

⅛ tsp. pepper

A pinch of paprika

1 Tbsp. fresh chives (for garnish)

Hit It:

Smile. Know that you're about to prepare the best mac and cheese ever!

Preheat oven to 350°. Grease a 13" x 9" nonstick metal baking pan with 2 Tbsp. butter. Prepare the macaroni according to the package directions, but make sure it's al dente. (**Huh?** It should still be a little firm.) Be sure to add a pinch of salt and a dash of olive oil to the boiling water while cooking. Drain pasta well and pour into the baking pan.

In a large mixing bowl, add the heavy cream, half-and-half, and sour cream; break the cream cheese into little bits with your (clean!) fingers as you add it to the bowl. Add the egg, flour, Worcestershire sauce, garlic and onion powders, mustard powder, cayenne pepper, nutmeg, salt, and pepper, combine very well with a wire whisk to break up that cream cheese. It will look lumpy, but that's okay.

Starting at the corners of the pasta dish, place and push down the Velveeta and white Vermont cheddar cubes. Work your way around and toward the middle (they won't push down completely, but just smoosh them down a bit). Now sprinkle the fabulous Gruyère cheese evenly over the top—gently and evenly pour that artery-clogging mixture on it, covering all areas. Gently shake the pan afterwards for a sec to make sure the liquid is even. I know it sounds gross, but push down and make little holes into areas of the mixture with your fingers. (You're just getting some of that Gruyère down deeper below

(Continued on next page)

the surface, and bringing some of that liquid *up* to the surface.) Wash your hands!

Sprinkle the jack-and-cheddar combo over this mixture and sprinkle the paprika on top. Put this baby in the oven (make sure your oven rack is right in the middle) and bake for approximately 30 minutes, or until it starts to get brownish and bubbly all over. It will be creamy in the center and more crusty on the top and edges. Chop some fresh chives and get those taste buds ready. When it's done, garnish with the chives (but try not to eat part of the crusty top before you serve it. I'm watching you!).

Get out of town! This is actually a one-way ticket to paradise.

Serves 10.

Carnie Aside-a:

For a super delish variation, omit the nutmeg and scatter ½ cup finely chopped onions and celery (that have been sautéed in 1 Tbsp. butter until clear) plus a 9-oz. packet of flaked white albacore tuna over the noodles before adding the cream mixture. Never mind what I said before—*this* is the best ever!

Chew on My Maque Choux

*For those of you who've never had maque choux, it's basically a creamy corn dish with bell peppers. It's fabulous with baked chicken dishes or the **Mock Cannelloni for My "Hony"** on page 100. Trust me.*

Stuff You Need:

2 Tbsp. unsalted butter

4 cups corn (about 6 ears), cut off the cob

1 sweet onion, chopped

Half of a red bell pepper, chopped

1 tsp. serrano chili, minced

½ tsp. paprika

½ tsp. garlic powder

¼ tsp. each: black pepper, onion powder, oregano, and thyme

1 tsp. salt

1 tsp. brown sugar

1 tsp. dried basil

1 Tbsp. fresh basil leaves, chopped

¼ cup chicken broth

½ tsp. lemon juice

2 tsp. flat-leaf parsley, freshly minced

½ cup heavy cream

Hit It:

Melt the butter in a large frying pan over medium-high heat. Add the corn, onions, bell peppers, chili, paprika, and herbs (but only half of the fresh basil and parsley), onion powder, and brown sugar; cook, stirring until soft, for 10 minutes. Add the cream and chicken broth and cook for 2 minutes; taste and correct seasoning. Add salt to taste. Remove from the heat, add the remaining fresh basil, garnish with parsley, and serve hot.

Serves 6.

Some Real Mean Beans

Stuff You Need:

Four 15-oz. cans small pink
  beans or pinto beans, rinsed

¾ cup olive oil

2 large white onions, finely chopped

4 cloves garlic, finely minced

3 large tomatoes, finely chopped

4 serrano chilis or jalapeños, finely
  chopped (reduce to 2 if you're
  serving the faint of stomach)

2 cups cilantro, finely chopped

Sea salt to taste

Juice of 2 limes

2–3 cups dark beer or stout

Hit It:

Heat the oil in a large, deep, heavy skillet over a medium-high heat. Add the onions and garlic; fry until lightly browned. Add the tomatoes, chilis, cilantro, cooked beans, salt, and beer; continue to cook, uncovered, over low heat until the mixture thickens, about 45 minutes. Pour the hot beans into a cool-looking ceramic serving dish. Mmm . . . perfect.

Serves 8.

Now Serving:

Match these mucho yummy beans with roasted meats and corn or flour tortillas.

Corn in the USA Pudding

Corn pudding holds a special place in my heart. If they somehow outlawed mac and cheese, it might even move up to number one on my list . . . or at least number two after mashed potatoes! Serve this dish all year 'round and enjoy. (Sometimes I even throw in a few diced green chilis—after all, you need to have a little spice in your life.)

Stuff You Need:

2 eggs, beaten

One 15-oz. can cream-style corn

One 8-oz. container sour cream

½ cup butter, melted

⅛ tsp. nutmeg

⅛ tsp. cayenne pepper

½ tsp. salt

1 Tbsp. brown sugar

1 lb. frozen sweet-corn kernels,
  thawed and drained

One 8.5-oz. pkg. dry corn-muffin mix
  (I like Jiffy brand)

Hit It:

Preheat oven to 350°. Grease a 2-quart casserole dish. In a large mixing bowl, combine the eggs, cream-style corn, sour cream, and melted butter. Add the corn kernels and seasonings; stir in the corn-muffin mix until just moistened. Bake for 45–55 minutes or until an inserted knife comes out clean and the top is golden. Let stand 5 minutes before serving.

Serves 8.

That's Amore: Stir-Fry Italian Veggies

Stuff You Need:

3 Tbsp. extra-virgin olive oil

1 cup sweet onions, sliced

2 cups fennel bulb, thinly sliced

1½ cups tender young green beans, sliced into 2″ pieces

2 cups rapini, trimmed (**Huh?** Rapini is Italian broccoli)

4 garlic cloves, minced

½ tsp. red pepper flakes

3 cups mushrooms, sliced (**Tip:** Try button mushrooms, shiitake, and portobellos, and mix 'em up—yum!)

2 large tomatoes, seeded and chopped into small pieces

1 tsp. fresh rosemary, minced

1 tsp. sea salt

⅛ cup dry white wine (optional)

½ cup fresh basil chiffonade

1 Tbsp. capers

1 Tbsp. balsamic vinegar

Freshly grated Parmesan shavings

Hit It:

Heat the olive oil in a large, wide sauté pan or wok; toss in the onion and stir for 2–3 minutes. Add the green beans, rapini, and fennel and stir for 3–4 minutes; add the garlic and pepper flakes. Add the mushrooms, salt, and rosemary, and continue to cook for 2–3 minutes. Add in all the remaining ingredients and continue to stir-fry until the vegetables are just tender and still brightly colored.

Serves 6–8.

Now Serving:

Transfer to a nicely warmed platter, drizzle with balsamic vinegar, and top with Parmesan shavings.

Broiled Tomatoes Two Healthy Ways

The Cheese-and-Bread-Crumb Way

Stuff You Need:

1½ lbs. (about 4) vine-ripened
    tomatoes, cut in half

2½ large garlic cloves, finely minced

½ cup dry bread crumbs

¼ cup grated Parmesan cheese

¼ cup each of the following: parsley,
    basil, and thyme, all finely minced

1 Tbsp. olive oil

2 Tbsp. melted butter

½ tsp. salt

½ tsp. freshly ground black pepper

Hit It:

Preheat broiler. Oil a shallow baking pan that's large enough to hold the tomatoes in one layer and arrange them inside, cut-side up. Mix the bread crumbs, Parmesan, herbs, salt, pepper, and garlic together in a small bowl; add the butter and olive oil and mix thoroughly. Spread ⅛ of the mixture on each tomato, and broil about 6–10 inches from the heat for 8 minutes, or until bubbling.

Serves 8.

The Skinny Cheese-and-Bread-Crumb Way

Stuff You Need:

1½ lbs. (about 4) vine-ripened
    tomatoes, cut in half

2½ large garlic cloves, finely minced

¼ cup dry bread crumbs

½ cup grated fat-free Parmesan cheese

¼ cup each of the following: parsley,
    basil, and thyme, all finely minced

1 tsp. olive oil

1 tsp. melted butter

½ tsp. salt

½ tsp. freshly ground black pepper

Pam or a nonstick cooking spray

Hit It:

Preheat broiler. Using Pam, spray a shallow baking pan large enough to hold the tomatoes in one layer and arrange them inside, cut-side up. Mix the bread crumbs, Parmesan, herbs, salt, pepper, and garlic together in a small bowl; add the butter and olive oil and mix thoroughly. Spread ⅛ of the mixture on each tomato, and broil about 6–10 inches from the heat for 8 minutes, or until bubbling

Serves 8.

Now Serving:

Either one of these tomato dishes is delicious with grilled meats or chicken.

Great Greek-Style Beans

Stuff You Need:

2 lbs. whole baby green beans, fresh or frozen (**Tip:** If you use the frozen ones, thaw and drain first.)

Juice of 1 lemon

1 Tbsp. dried mint

3 Tbsp. tomato paste

3 Tbsp. extra-virgin olive oil

1 sweet onion, finely chopped

1 tsp. sugar

1 tsp. salt (or to taste)

⅛ tsp. cayenne pepper

⅔ cup warm water

Hit It:

In a deep skillet or large Dutch oven, sauté the onion in olive oil until translucent. Stir in the tomato paste, salt, sugar, cayenne pepper, and mint; add the water and heat thoroughly. Add the green beans. (**Tip:** Using tongs to avoid breaking them, lift and gently toss the beans until they're coated with the tomato mixture.) Cover and cook on medium heat for 10–15 minutes or until the beans are tender but still retain their bright green color. Remove from the heat and toss with lemon juice.

Serves 8.

Now Serving:

You can dish these babies up hot or at room temperature. I love that you can also make this dish in advance—which is a time-saver if you're having friends over for dinner, but you have to work that day. I also love it with chicken. Opa!

Marti's Zucchini Soufflé

This makes a huge batch, but don't worry—it will go fast.

Stuff You Need:

6–8 medium zucchini

8 eggs

2 cups Bisquick Lite

¾ cup canola oil

½ cup onion, chopped

½ tsp. dried oregano

1 tsp. dried parsley

¾ tsp. salt

½ tsp. black pepper

Hit It:

Preheat oven to 350°. Clean and then grate the zucchini in a food processor. (**Tip:** Don't puree, just grate.) Combine with all the other ingredients in a large bowl; transfer to a 9" x 13" Pyrex dish and cook for 45–60 minutes or until a knife inserted into the center of soufflé comes out clean.

Serves 10.

Now Serving:

This is a great side for almost any dinner entrée. When it doubt, just serve it.

Curry Me Away
(Cauliflower and Broccoli Mix)

You might need to be "curried" to bed after this one because it's very rich.

Stuff You Need:

1½ lbs. each, broccoli and cauliflower florets, cooked (microwave each on high in a Ziploc bag with 2 Tbsp. water for 4 minutes)

1 cup light sour cream

½ cup plain low-fat yogurt

¼ cup nonfat milk

1 cup mayonnaise

3 Tbsp. curry powder

½ tsp. sugar

1 Tbsp. lemon juice

½ tsp. salt

½ tsp. black pepper

2 scallions (use about 3" of the green stem), trimmed and thinly sliced

8 oz. 2% cheddar cheese, shredded

8 oz. American cheese, cubed

½ cup grated Parmesan cheese

Hit It:

In a large mixing bowl, blend the sour cream, mayo, yogurt, and nonfat milk. Add the curry powder, sugar, lemon juice, salt, pepper, and scallions; fold in the American cheese and grated Parmesan and set aside.

Place the broccoli and cauliflower, a flew florets at a time, into a Crock-Pot. Using a spatula, pour the sour-cream mixture over the veggies, gently distributing it evenly. Cook on low for about 6 hours. Sprinkle with the cheddar cheese about 25 minutes before serving and replace cover.

Serves 12.

Ro-Ro-Roast Your Veggies

Nothing represents fall for me like the smell of veggies roasting in the oven. There's a sweetness that fills the air (and my mouth) that's better than any bottled perfume. It just says "home". . . .

Stuff You Need:

¾ pound tiny Yukon gold potatoes (or larger thin-skinned potatoes), unpeeled and cut into ¼" slices

½ lb. pearl onions, peeled

3 large carrots, peeled, cut in half lengthwise and then into 2" chunks

½ lb. baby portobello or large button mushrooms

1 fennel bulb, halved lengthwise and cut into ½"-wide wedges through the core

¾ pound asparagus, tough ends trimmed and cut into 2" lengths

2 zucchini, ends trimmed, halved lengthwise, and cut into ½"-thick slices

3 Japanese eggplant, ends trimmed, sliced into ½"-thick coins

1 large acorn squash, sliced in half separating top from bottom, seeded, and cut into six to eight ½"-thick rings

½ cup extra-virgin olive oil

3 cloves garlic, finely minced

Sea salt and freshly ground black pepper to taste

Hit It:

Preheat oven to 425°. In a small dish, add the garlic to the olive oil and let sit for at least an hour. Line a deep roasting pan with foil and toss all of the cut vegetables into it, separating them if possible; drizzle the olive-oil-and-garlic mixture over the vegetables, tossing well to distribute (you may not need to use all of it). Sprinkle sea salt over all. Place the pan in the oven, roasting the root vegetables and squash for 45 minutes. Remove from the oven and add the other, softer-skinned vegetables. Return to the oven and roast until all of the vegetables are glossy and caramelized. (**Tip:** This should take about another 40 minutes.) Every 10 minutes, move the veggies around with tongs to avoid breakage and to ensure that they cook evenly.

Serves 8.

Now Serving:

This dish can be served hot immediately or let rest at room temperature to enjoy later. Serve it up with anything!

Carnie Aside-a:

You can actually have fun while chopping veggies. Put on a Billie Holiday or Ella Fitzgerald CD, and *wheeeeeee!* Suddenly, you're chop, chop, chopping to the classics.

A Hill of Beans
(Green Beans with Lemon and Dill)

This is a very simple but delicious way to prepare your green beans. I love to serve this yummy dish with meat, chicken, and fish.

Stuff You Need:

1 lb. green beans, trimmed
   and washed

1–2 Tbsp. butter or I Can't
   Believe It's Not Butter

½ of a lemon

1 Tbsp. fresh dill or 1 tsp. dried dill

⅛ tsp. sugar

Kosher salt and pepper to taste

Hit It:

Steam the green beans in a colander, covered, over boiling water for approximately 10 minutes or until pretty soft when pierced with a fork. Throw the beans into a large sauté pan that's been heated with the butter. Squeeze the lemon juice over the beans, sprinkle on the sugar and dill, and toss well in the pan. Cook until heated through, and season with salt and pepper

Serves 4–6.

Oh, Baby Carrots

This is another great side for meat, chicken, and fish . . . mmm.

Stuff You Need:

1 pkg. baby carrots

1 Tbsp. butter

1 tsp. brown sugar

1½ tsp. fresh chopped dill

Kosher salt and freshly ground
   black pepper to taste

Hit It:

Place the carrots in a colander or steamer basket in a saucepan with 2" boiling water; cover the pan with foil or a tight-fitting lid, and cook until tender, approximately 7–10 minutes.

Melt the butter in a 10" skillet on medium heat. Add the carrots, chopped dill, and sugar; salt and pepper to taste. Sauté until heated through. Congratulate yourself for eating your veggies!

Serves 6.

Broc On (Hot Broccoli Mold)

This is the perfect side dish to make you smile!

Stuff You Need:

Two 10-oz. pkgs. frozen chopped broccoli, cooked and drained well

¼ cup chicken or turkey broth

3 Tbsp. butter

¼ cup scallions

3 Tbsp. all-purpose flour

½ cup mayonnaise

3 eggs, lightly beaten

⅓ cup Swiss cheese

¼ cup Gruyère cheese

½ tsp. nutmeg

1 tsp. salt

¼ tsp. black pepper

¼ cup toasted almonds, finely chopped

3 Tbsp. pimentos, chopped

Hit It:

Preheat oven to 350°. Generously grease a 5-cup ring mold. In a medium-size bowl, add the chicken or turkey broth to the cooked broccoli; set aside. Melt the butter in a large saucepan, add the scallions, and sauté until tender. Mix in the flour and cook, stirring constantly for about one minute. Blend in the sour cream and cook, stirring constantly until thick. (**Tip:** Do not boil.) Remove from the heat and add the eggs. Stir in the broccoli-broth mixture, cheeses, seasonings, nuts, and pimento. Pour the mixture into the mold and place it in a shallow dish of boiling water. Carefully place the mold and the dish in the oven, and bake for 45 minutes or until a knife inserted comes out clean. Let it stand 5 minutes . . . if you can keep your hands off it, that is.

Run a knife around the edges to loosen, and then "un-mold." Slice and serve as a fabulous side dish for dinner, and let the love rock your world.

Serves 8.

Steamed Spinach . . . Not!
(It's Creamed Spinach)

Stuff You Need:

Two 9-oz. bags fresh, prewashed baby spinach leaves

1 Tbsp. olive oil

2 cloves garlic, minced

One 8-oz. pkg. cream cheese (at room temp.)

2 tsp. lemon juice

4 scallions (with about 3″ of the tender green stem), sliced thinly

Lawry's Seasoned Salt and freshly ground black pepper to taste

Hit It:

In a large, deep sauté pan, heat the olive oil and sauté the garlic for about 2 minutes. Toss in the scallions and stir for about 1 minute; add the spinach and stir until it's wilted and reduced in volume, about 3 minutes. Cut the cream cheese into cubes and toss into the pan with the lemon juice. Stir until the cream cheese is melted and thoroughly mixed into spinach. Add Lawry's and pepper to taste.

Serves 6.

CHAPTER SEVEN

The Parents Are Coming! I'm Making Him Dinner for the First Time!— Situational Cooking 101

Here's the first rule when it comes to having company: *It's not about perfection.* In fact, the idea of messing up a little bit is just part of the fun, which is the basic idea of having your friends and loved ones over. Remember that entertaining should be fun. Read that sentence again. Now, say it loud and proud. Are you almost convinced?

To take that lost feeling out of entertaining for others, I'm going to give you a few beautiful road maps in this chapter. Remember that you're allowed to swerve off of them and follow your own path. There are no rules. Just do what makes you feel good, and I promise that your guests will follow right along.

Situation #1:

You're Making Your Significant Other Your First Home-Cooked Meal Together

You've done the two or three great restaurant dinners where it's been about gazing into each other's eyes and not eating much of what's on your plate. Now it's time for a bold move, which is to cook for the guy or girl you like at your home. This isn't the time to panic, but rather to prepare for a lovely evening of firsts. How many firsts are up to you. I'm just talking about the first time you get out pots and pans for this special person!

THE MENU

Appetizer: Gloria's Butter-You-Up Butternut-Squash Soup (page 50).

Entrée: Poached Salmon with Unforgetta Bruschetta (page 97).

Sides: Righteous Mashed Potatoes with Roasted Garlic (page 108), steamed broccoli, and steamed asparagus.

Dessert: You. (Just kidding—I like Häagen-Dazs sorbet.) You don't need to cook every course on the first big dinner date at your house. Buying some yummy ice cream makes everyone happy. Plus, you can feed each other a bite. You can also do a lemon sorbet with fresh raspberries, strawberries, and blueberries. Cut them up in front of your date and feed each other the stray berries. Add a little bit of sugar and lemon juice to the fruit medley before pouring it on the sorbet. It makes you look like a cooking whiz. If you want to go extra sinful for dessert, you can make my **Sweetie Pie** (page141) and become the light of his or her eye.

To Drink: May I suggest a Pinot Grigio or a gorgeous Chardonnay? If he or she doesn't drink alcohol, then a specialty iced tea with a hint of peach or raspberry would be great.

For the Table: Beautiful peach-colored roses with red tips, pretty unscented candles, and your best china or plates. I really love place mats, and I don't care if they come from Tiffany or Target. Cloth napkins, napkin rings, and good silver (if you have it) are also wonderful touches.

For Your Ears: Sade's albums *Stronger Than Pride* or *Love Deluxe; Fields of Gold: The Best of Sting 1984–1994;* or anything from Barry White or Marvin Gaye. Annie Lennox—any album she's ever done—will also do.

Added Touch: Perfume sprayed behind your ears (my favorite is Clinique Happy).

Time to Create a Scene: Two hours.

Hint: It's all about the prep. Read all the recipes—*all the way through*—before you even pick up a spoon. Have your ingredients measured out and available. And remember that timing is everything.

So You Messed Up: Let's say that you overcooked the salmon and you're worried that it's going to be a little bit dry. Don't despair: Because you're cooking the fish in liquid, it's not as dry as you think (still, you want it to be soft in the center). And remember that the tomato flavor of the bruschetta will mask any issue with the fish. Remember that you and your date are both eating garlic here, so it won't matter if you choose to kiss each other later—you'll both be carrying the scent of a good Italian restaurant. Believe me, the flavor of garlic will be in your mouth until the next day.

Situation #2:

Your Parents or In-laws Are Coming for Dinner

This is not the time to move out of the country! You must face the fact that you're an adult now, which means that at some point you're going to have to put some grub on the table for your relatives. No, slamming down a pizza box from Domino's and saying, "Eat up" just won't do. Of course, I absolutely realize that you'll be under serious scrutiny here—just take a deep breath, and let's hit it!

THE MENU

Appetizers: Your folks may want to eat the minute they get there. A fabulous cheese tray decorated with red grapes, apricots, giant berries, almonds, black olives, prosciutto, and cheeses such as Havarti, Swiss, cheddar, and jack is perfect for nibbles. Serve with a nice tray of crackers.

Another great starter is **Holy Guacamole** (page 69) with chips, which never fails. Or you can just create a tray of gourmet cheeses, olives, and fancy crackers. You can also serve them my **Hot Chickpea Dip** (page 74) with pita chips—I love this with fresh pita bread, too. Either way, the parents will be impressed!

Entrée: Perfect Breasts and Thighs (page 84) is so easy, especially if you're nervous about this meal; **Yeah, It's Oy Vey Brisket** (page 89) is also a fabulous choice. Seafood lovers will adore **Just for the Halibut** (page 98). And everyone will love **Chicken Cacciatore If You Can** (page 81).

Sides: If you do the chicken or brisket, I'd suggest **Righteous Mashed Potatoes with Roasted Garlic** (page 108) and **Oh, Baby Carrots** (page 127) or simple steamed asparagus. You can also do the **Oh-So-Nice Baked Rice** (page 114) instead of mashed potatoes. If you do the fish, it could be an "ocean fest" if you start with the **Tuna Tartare** (page 55). Serve the halibut with a green salad, mashed potatoes, and **Great Greek-Style Beans** (page 123).

Dessert: I love to serve **Hawaiian Lu-*aah* Sundaes** (page 156) to my parents or in-laws because they bring out the kid inside everyone. Another great choice is **Sweetie Pie** (page 141), a dish that really impresses. (Plus, it's so easy and quick!) You can also totally knock 'em out with **Come Together Pudding** (page 136).

If your guests are health nuts, just serve them some mixed berries with freshly whipped cream (1 cup cream plus one Tbsp. sugar and ½ tsp. vanilla).

To Drink: Wine is great, especially if your guests bring it! I'd also provide sodas and iced tea, along with ice water with fresh lemon slices.

For the Table: Flowers are essential, but you can pick up a mixed bunch from that guy who sells them next to the highway—you don't have to spend big bucks to make it pretty. (My favorite thing to do for these kinds of events is to cut some roses from my own yard. That way, when someone admires them, I can take them out and show them the garden.) Just be sure that the bouquet is low enough on the table that your guests can see each other.

This is also a great time to get out all the good stuff: the wedding china, the silver, and the lovely candlesticks. Light some unscented candles, even if it's a 90-degree day. They always make a room so pretty!

Extra: Have a family photo album handy. You might be shocked at how much you enjoy taking a trek down memory lane.

For Your Ears: I'm partial to standards when I have parents visit (anything from Billie Holiday works well, too). I also like to ask my guests in advance what their favorite music is. In other words, this is usually not the time for Eminem.

Way to Get Your Mom Out of the Kitchen While You're Cooking: Say with love, "Mom this is your night to relax. Let me do everything."

When This Doesn't Work: Let her help. She loves it, and you can tolerate it.

Situation #3:

You Just Had a Huge Fight and Want to Make Up

Just in case Rob and I ever really get into it, I plan on appealing to his stomach as a make-up tool . . .

THE MENU

Appetizers: Getta Some Bruschetta (page 52), along with the words, "Honey, I love you and I hate when we fight. I'm going to make you a beautiful dinner. But while you wait, enjoy my homemade bruschetta. After all, that's the kind of wife/husband/ partner I am—I care about you and your late-afternoon hunger pangs." You can also serve **Don't Mean to Boast about This Pink Toast** (page 60). Pop one in his or her mouth and watch him or her come back two or three times for you—I mean more.

Entrée: Perfect Breasts and Thighs (page 84). It really is perfect—for any situation!

Sides: Baja Rice Bake (page 115) because it sounds like a vacation spot, as in, "Let's spend a romantic weekend in Baja someday." Serve with **That's Amore: Stir-Fry Italian Veggies** (page 121) for obvious reasons.

For Your Ears: Well, this is not the time to put on "You're No Good" by Wilson Phillips, even if that's what you're thinking! And while I like Michael Jackson's "Wanna Be Startin' Somethin'," that song could conceivably bring up old issues. But "Tonight, Tonight, Tonight" by Genesis, with the refrain of "we're gonna make it right" seems to make sense.

For the Table: It's nice to have a cozy dinner in the kitchen when you're making up. But clear the books or magazines off the table—you don't need any distractions now. And turn the phone and TV off!

Extras: Hopefully, he'll run out and get you some "I screwed up" flowers.

Dessert: I'll Crumble for You (page 143) will hit every spot. How could it be bad?

Situation #4:

Girls' Night In!

It's just like when we were kids: No boys allowed.

I love an evening in with the girls, and I'm always trying to make it special. One thing is for sure: Guys don't always appreciate the little extra touches, but girls kvell over them. (Oh, *kvell* is a Yiddish way of saying "Lose your mind.")

THE MENU

Appetizer: A big bowl of **Break Your Heartichoke Dip** (page 70) served with fat-free crackers and pita strips. In case one of you is brokenhearted, it's a good way to gather 'round the dip and dish.

Entrée: A Lotta Chicken Enchilada Casserole (page 87).

Sides: Some Real Mean Beans (page 119) and **Baja Rice Bake** (page 115). ¡Olé!

Dessert: This is tricky. I like to make **Everybody Was Tofu Biting** (page 153) because it's a sugar-free chocolate mousse—this way, even your most diet-conscious friends will be able to have a few bites. I also like the **Dump Cake** (page 150), just in case you might be sitting around dumping on someone or just gossiping in general.

For the Table: Forget the flowers—just have the latest *In Style* and *Us Weekly* handy. Read the stories about Tom Cruise and Brad Pitt aloud. With great drama, deliver the quotes about how they just can't seem to find the right women. (Obviously because they're in your kitchen!)

For Your Ears: I like Aretha Franklin's *30 Greatest Hits* or any disco music by Donna Summer. It's perfectly acceptable and wonderful to dance around the kitchen in your socks.

Extras: Have the girls bring their pj's. Change into them when you're ready, and watch a really drippy movie like *Beaches* (have tons of Kleenex handy). Try to convince yourself that Barbara Hershey really might not die this time . . . and gawk at the size of her lips.

Situation #5:
No One's Coming Over, I'm Depressed, and I Think I'll Cook for Myself

We've all been there, but my suggestion is that you don't just open a can or eat out of a box. There's nothing nicer than being nice to yourself. You deserve it.

THE MENU

Appetizer: I know you're not going to make one for yourself, but the **Get Your Greens Spinach Salad** (with **Raspberry Dressing**) on page 31 is nice and easy.

Entrée: Rob's Mom's Split-Pea Soup (page 47). It's so comforting; plus you'll get an extra dose of pleasure by having a piece of crusty bread with it. **Tuna Canoodle** (page 99) is another great, easy dish to make, and you can share the leftovers with family and neighbors.

But let's say that you've had a really hard day. I say go for it and make **Fall to Your Knees Mac and Cheese** (page 117). The cool thing here is that no one will know how much of it you ate.

For Your Ears: Please don't put on Eric Carmen's "All by Myself"—it's the saddest song I've ever heard in my life! Also avoid Three Dog Night's "One." I say you should put on something loud like "Wake Me Up Before You Go-Go" or "Bad Boys" by Wham!

Extras: I love supermarket flowers—they're cheap, easy joy.

CHAPTER EIGHT

Mmm, Shut Up—
The Most
Fab Desserts

Now that we've got the hard stuff out of the way, it's time for the best chapter of all. In fact, perhaps we should call it "Til' Dessert Do Us Part." Yet, as someone who's lost more than 150 pounds, I know how to have my low-fat cake and lose weight, too.

Without further ado, here's the good stuff. (P.S. Believe me, it's *all* good!)

Come Together Pudding:
THE SINFUL

Okay, all I can say is, "Get your mouth ready for this one," because it's one of the greatest things I've ever eaten. It's also perfect for a dinner party or potluck. In fact, nobody will believe that you made it, and you'll probably burn off several calories in a heated discussion about that very fact. And if you make this during the holidays, people will lose their minds. My mouth is watering just thinking about it. . . .

Now for the reality check: This dessert requires a little bit of work, but don't get scared. It's also a little messy, but you'll get a bit of a workout. In fact, you'll probably work up a little sweat by just looking at it.

My inspiration for this recipe came from the amazing cookbook author and chef Paula Deen. (I added the dulce de leche caramel sauce, which should be drizzled with the chocolate, and the peanut butter.) Thank you, Paula—you're a goddess. I can't wait to visit you in Savannah at your Lady & Sons restaurant. For the rest of you out there who can't take the trip, just make this dessert. Eat it and weep . . . or eat it and work out the next day. (By the way, we're talking two bites of this baby for the gastric-bypass patient.)

P.S. This dessert is best if it's prepared five hours to one day in advance. And make sure that you wait to drizzle the caramel and chocolate sauce just before you serve it.

Stuff You Need:

1 box Nilla wafers

4 bananas, sliced (**Tip:** They should be ripe.)

One 3.5-oz. box vanilla instant-pudding mix

One 14-oz. can sweetened condensed milk *(mmm)*

1 cup milk

1 cup heavy whipping cream

1 cup sour cream

16 teaspoon-sized dots of peanut butter (⅓–½ cup)

½ cup Hershey's chocolate, or hot-fudge sauce, melted (for drizzling)

½ cup Smucker's dulce de leche caramel sauce, melted (for drizzling)— is there anything more yummy?

(Pepcid. You'll need it later if you have a big portion. Ha ha!)

Hit It:

In a big mixing bowl, combine the pudding, condensed milk, and milk. Stir vigorously, or use a mixer and beat for 2 minutes. Place in the refrigerator for 10 minutes.

In another bowl, whip the heavy cream until stiff peaks form. Mix it and the sour cream into the pudding mixture until well combined. Put ½ the Nilla wafers on the bottom of a 13" x 9" x 3" pan, and put ½ the sliced bananas on top; dollop the peanut butter in 4 even rows of 4 dots over this. Spread ½ the pudding mixture over the bananas and cookies, drizzle ½ the caramel and chocolate sauce over the pudding; repeat layers, ending with the sauces.

Realistically, this serves 10 people. But people go back for more . . . and more . . . and more. It's also great the next morning—if there's any left (which is almost never).

Come Together Pudding:
THE SKINNY

Just Substitute the Following:

Sugar-free pudding mix

Low-fat milk

Fat-free sour cream

Reduced-fat Nilla wafers

Fat-free chocolate sauce

Low-fat peanut butter

Carnie Aside-a:
Omit the peanut butter and substitute with sliced strawberries, and it gets even skinnier.

Angelico Frangelico Chocolate Bread Pudding

Frangelico is a hazelnut-flavored liqueur, but if you don't like it, you can easily omit it. Please serve this dish warm with vanilla ice cream—and then put me in a cage.

Stuff You Need:

1 loaf crusty bakery bread, cut into 1″ cubes (about 1 lb., or 15 cups)

2½ cups whole milk

½ cup half-and-half

¼ cup Frangelico

1½ cups white sugar

½ cup light brown sugar

¼ cup Dutch cocoa powder (**Tip:** Use Droste brand or similar. It isn't the same with regular cocoa powder like Hershey's.)

1 Tbsp. vanilla extract

1 tsp. cinnamon

½ tsp. nutmeg

6 large eggs, lightly beaten

8 oz. semisweet chocolate (my favorite is Scharffen Berger), grated (**Tip:** The grating is a pain in the you-know-where and sort of messy but *do it* . . . trust me!)

Dulce de leche caramel sauce for drizzling

Hit It:

Preheat oven to 325°. Place the bread cubes in a lightly greased 13″ x 9″ Pyrex dish. Whisk together the milk, half-and-half, and Frangelico in a large mixing bowl. In a second bowl, combine the sugars and cocoa powder until well combined; add to the milk mixture and whisk until combined. Add the vanilla, cinnamon, and nutmeg to the beaten eggs; combine the egg and the milk mixtures in the larger of the two bowls and whisk until incorporated.

Add the grated chocolate, and pour the mixture evenly over the bread cubes. Let sit, stirring occasionally, for at least 15 minutes or until the bread has absorbed most of the milk mixture.

Place the pan in the oven and bake for about an hour, or until the pudding has set. (**Tip:** This is when a knife inserted in the center comes out clean.) Let the pudding rest for 5 minutes, then drizzle lots of the caramel sauce in a zigzag pattern over the top. Serve warm or chilled—either way it's not to be believed!

Serves 10–12.

Berry, Berry Delicious Bars

*This is Rob's favorite dessert, which I still can't believe he likes better than **Come Together Pudding.** Oh well, to each his own . . . dessert.*

Stuff You Need:

1 cup butter, softened

1 cup sugar

1 egg

½ tsp. vanilla

2 cups flour

¾ cup walnuts, coarsely chopped

One 10-oz. jar seedless raspberry
    or strawberry preserves

For the Icing:

1 cup powdered sugar, sifted

2 Tbsp. milk

¼ tsp. vanilla

¼ tsp. almond extract or
    ½ tsp. lemon juice

Hit It:

Preheat oven to 350°. In a medium bowl, beat the butter and sugar with an electric mixer on medium speed until combined, light, and fluffy. (**Tip:** Don't forget to scrape down the sides of the bowl a few times while you're doing this because it will get all the butter lumps out and make an even mixture.) Add the egg and vanilla; beat in as much flour as you can with the mixer; if there's any remaining, mix it by hand. (**Tip:** When finished blending with the mixer, you'll want to get your ingredients off the blades. You can slow down the speed and slowly lift the blades out of the mixture when you're finished. All the ingredients will fall off, but be careful not to splatter.) Stir in the walnut pieces. Set aside 1 cup of this dough mixture.

Press the dough (minus the 1 cup we set aside) into an ungreased 9" x 9" x 2" baking pan. Spread the preserves on, leaving a ½" border of dough. Take the reserved dough and dot it on top of the preserves. Bake for 45 minutes or until the top is golden brown; cool on a wire rack.

In a small bowl, combine the ingredients for the icing, adding additional milk if necessary to thin it. Drizzle the icing on the bars and cut them into 4" squares. Watch everyone flip out, lose their minds, and go bananas—even though we're dealing with berries here (you get the idea).

Serves 8–10.

Tears for My Pillows
(S'mores Croissants)

Stuff You Need:

¼ cup butter (or ½ stick)

1½ cups chopped nuts
  (walnuts, almonds, or whatever you prefer)

6 graham crackers

1 pkg. crescent-roll dough

12 large marshmallows

½ cup semisweet chocolate chips

Hit It:

Melt the butter and chop the nuts. Coarsely break up the graham crackers and set aside in a small bowl. We're creating an assembly line now. (This is really fun for kids, so involve them in this one.)

Pop and separate the dough into its pre-cut triangle pieces, and spray some cupcake pans with Pam. Roll the marshmallows in the butter and nuts and place in the center of one of the individual crescent rolls. Take each end of the triangle and, overlapping the dough over the marshmallow, pinch the bottom (but leave the top open); place in the cupcake tin. When finished with all 12 crescent-roll "pillows," put a pinch of graham cracker and a pinch of the chocolate on top.

Makes 12.

Sweetie Pie

Here's an embarrassing story about me and pie. Every summer when I was a teenager, I was shipped off to Weight Watchers camp with my cousin Jonah. Let's just say that we weren't exactly roasting marshmallows by the fire. But we did make pie one day as an exercise on how to create a healthy dessert and then use restraint while eating it.

The same night that the camp made pies for our cooking class, Jonah and I staged a midnight break-in. (I'm ratting him out, finally—Jonah broke the lock. I'm totally innocent on that part!) I followed him into the kitchen in the dark with a flashlight. Once inside, we not only ate some of our pies, but the several other delicious varieties that were just sitting there on the shelf as well. The next day, they held a camp meeting: All the campers had to gather in the auditorium and wait until someone broke down and fessed up. Jonah and I never uttered a word—until now. Are we sorry? No, we were desperate. But we can say "Sorry" to Susan, the camp nutritionist. We know she was mortified, and we're still working on repenting.

These days, I don't feel so guilty about pies, especially the great one below. Just knowing that it's there and not under lockdown helps me find the willpower to have just a few bites. I mean, if you're gonna splurge, you might as well get maximum joy. (Oh, you've really gotta like chocolate and caramel here.) Anyway, here's a way to send yourself into the stratosphere. In fact, I think I'll make one for Jonah right now.

Quick thanks: This is chef and author Paula Deen's recipe, and it's outstanding.

Stuff You Need:

4 king-sized Snickers bars

½ cup peanut butter

1½ Tbsp. half-and-half

4 cups frozen whipped topping (such as Cool Whip), thawed

1 deep-dish, 9" graham-cracker crust

Additional whipped topping and Hershey's chocolate syrup for garnish. (**Tip:** It spreads germs to drink it out of the bottle. Remind yourself of this fact—it might help.)

Hit It:

In the top of a double boiler, melt together the Snickers bars, peanut butter, and half-and-half, stirring until smooth. Remove from heat and allow to cool slightly. Fold in the whipped topping, pour into the crust, and freeze for 4–6 hours before serving. When ready to serve, top with additional whipped topping and drizzle with chocolate syrup. Store in the refrigerator.

If you're a Snickers lover, this will *rock your world*.

Serves 8.

I'll Crumble for You
(Fresh Pear Cheesecake)

This recipe is from my friend and genius pastry chef George Geary. He has a book called 125 Best Cheesecake Recipes, and let me tell you something . . . he rocks! I asked him to give me a cheesecake with fresh fruit and a crumble top, and here's what he graciously sent to my kitchen.

Stuff You Need for the Crust:

1¼ cups graham-cracker crumbs

½ cup pecans, crushed

3 Tbsp. unsalted butter, melted

For the Topping:

1 cup all-purpose flour

½ cup oatmeal

½ cup light brown sugar, packed

2 Tbsp. granulated sugar

½ cup unsalted butter, cold and in chunks

½ tsp. ground cinnamon

¼ tsp. salt

For the Filling:

Four 8-oz. pkgs. cream cheese, softened

1¼ cups light brown sugar, packed

4 eggs

1 Tbsp. vanilla

1 tsp. fresh lemon juice

2 pears, peeled, cut, cored, and thinly sliced

Hit It:

Preheat oven to 350°. In a medium bowl, mix the crumbs, pecans, and butter. Press into the bottom of a 10" cheesecake pan and freeze uncovered until the filling is ready. Now make the topping.

In the bowl of a food processor, pulse (blend lightly) the flour, oatmeal, and sugars together until combined; add the butter and pulse 20 more times. Add the cinnamon and salt; pulse 5 more times and then set aside. It's time for the yummy filling!

In a large mixing bowl, beat the cream cheese and brown sugar with a hand mixer until creamy. Add the eggs, one at a time, and beat on medium-high for 3 minutes; add the lemon juice and vanilla, mixing until blended. Pour over the crust, smoothing it until it touches the sides of the pan.

Arrange the pears in a spiral fashion over the filling and place the topping over the pears. Bake for 45–55 minutes or until it starts to pull away from the sides of the pan, but is still a bit loose in the center and looks puffy. Cool on a rack for 2 hours, then cover with plastic wrap and refrigerate for at least 2 more hours before serving.

Serves 12–14.

Losing Your Marbles Over Chocolate Cheesecake with Brownie Crust

Stuff You Need:

One 15-oz. pkg. fat-free fudge
  brownie mix

½ tsp. almond extract

2 tsp. instant espresso

1 individual-serving
  container (4 oz.) natural
  applesauce (no sugar added)

¾ cup sugar

1 Tbsp. flour

2 tsp. vanilla

One 8-oz. pkg. cream
  cheese, softened

One 8-oz. pkg. fat-free
  cream cheese, softened

2 egg whites (or 1½ egg equivalent
  of Egg Beaters or similar product)

3 Tbsp. 1% milk

2 Tbsp. Dutch cocoa (**Tip:** Use Droste
  brand or similar. It isn't the same with
  regular cocoa powder like Hershey's.)

Hit It:

Preheat oven to 425°. Blend the brownie mix, espresso powder, almond extract, and applesauce together; let sit for 20 minutes. Lightly spray the entire interior of a 9" springform pan with Pam. Using your fingertips, press the brownie mixture onto the bottom and 1"–2" up the side of the pan. Using a hand mixer at medium speed, beat the sugar, flour, vanilla, and cream cheese in a medium-size mixing bowl until smooth. Add the egg whites and beat for 2 minutes.

In a separate, smaller bowl, combine ½ cup of the batter with the cocoa and stir until incorporated. Place dollops of the remaining batter alternately with the cocoa batter into the prepared pan. Lightly swirl using the tip of a knife, being careful not to disturb the crust. (**Tip:** Don't overdo it or you won't get the marbled effect we want here.) Bake for 15 minutes; reduce oven temperature to 250°, and continue to bake for 45 minutes or until set. Cool completely before removing from the pan, and refrigerate for 2 hours or more. Prepare to lose your marbles.

Serves 8.

Beware of the Brownies
(Fudgy, Make-Your-Belly-Pudgy Brownies)

These four-layer brownies are totally decadent. They remind me of a chewy, frosted cake, and the peanut butter makes them off the hook! To send someone you love to places they've never been, serve these warm with some vanilla ice cream. Oh, Mama. . . .

Stuff You Need for the First Layer:

1 cup butter

⅓ cup Hershey's (or your favorite brand) cocoa

2 cups sugar (Lord help us!)

4 eggs

1½ cups flour

½ tsp. salt

1 tsp. vanilla

For the Second Layer:

1¼ cups chunky peanut butter (I use Skippy)

For the Third Layer (the Gene Frosting):

½ cup butter

¼ cup Hershey's cocoa

⅓ cup whole milk

8 large marshmallows (this is the gene part)

½ tsp. salt

1 tsp. vanilla

One 16-oz. box powdered sugar, sifted (**Huh?** Put through a small-mesh sieve and "tap through" until there are no lumps.)

For the Fourth Layer:

Caramel sauce, melted

Chopped pecans and almonds

Hit It:

Preheat oven to 350°. Grease a 13" x 9" x 2" pan with butter. (Now's the time to turn back if you're too afraid of the calories!) For the first layer, melt the cup of butter and cocoa in a double boiler. (**Tip:** You can also use a heat-proof bowl or a saucepan sitting over another that contains simmering water, or use a microwave.) Remove from the heat and cool. Blend in the sugar, eggs, and vanilla; combine with the flour and salt and add to the chocolate mixture. Mix to combine until there are no big lumps; pour into the greased pan and bake for 20–30 minutes. It will rise a little, and when you poke the center with a toothpick, it should come out just about clean. But *do not overbake:* You want these puppies moist!

Now, for the second layer: Spoon the peanut butter over the hot cake and spread it evenly while it's melting. (**For-Your-Hips Tip:** Don't eat any yet. Let it cool—I mean it!)

In a small saucepan, melt the butter, cocoa, milk, and marshmallows; add the salt and vanilla. Beat in the powdered sugar until it's totally combined with no lumps. (This is where I start to drool, but not in the pan!) Spread this third layer over the cooled peanut butter and check your pulse.

Finally, drizzle the heated caramel sauce over the frosting and sprinkle with nuts if desired. Cut into squares the size of your choice and quickly shove into your mouth.

Makes 12 large brownies or 16 medium ones.

145

Renee's "Banana Wonder" Bread
(with Banana Frosting)

There are wonderful things that we inherit from our parents: their kindness, sense of humor, or wisdom . . . and then there's banana bread.

On a cold winter night during the course of writing this book, my friend Cindy was searching through the kitchen cabinets at her father's home when she unearthed a family treasure. It was a tiny metal box filled with neatly preserved 3" x 5" index cards. On each of the yellowed cards was a beautifully handwritten recipe that her mother, Renee, had created during the course of her 30 years of married life. The recipes tell a story: There were the briskets, the Jell-O molds at Thanksgiving, that horrible fried liver that stank up the house and was fed to Bear, the big German shepherd, under the table . . . these recipes are a family autobiography.

Renee lost a battle to cancer at age 53. On those little cards are an inheritance more precious than all the jewels in the world. I've said it before, but the taste, the feel, and the smell of the foods we've loved and shared with our loved ones—well, that doesn't have anything to do with the stomach. Those are the moments that fill my heart.

Stuff You Need:

½ cup butter, softened

2 cups sugar

2 very ripe bananas (with some spots)

2 eggs, separated (yolks from whites)

1 cup sour cream

1 tsp. baking soda

2 tsp. baking powder

3 cups sifted flour

Hit It:

Preheat oven to 350°. Mix the butter and sugar together; add the bananas and beat well. Add only the egg yolks, one at a time, and beat well. Add the baking soda and half of the the sour cream; then add the flour and baking powder. Blend the rest of the sour cream into the batter. (**Tip:** When you're baking, remember to continually scrape down the sides of the bowl. This is not for a snack for the cook—it's important because things get stuck if you don't mix and scrape at the same time.) Gradually add the flour mixture. Beat the egg whites until they're stiff, and add to the batter. Pour the mixture into a greased 13" x 9" pan and bake for 35 minutes.

Serves 8–10.

Banana Frosting

Stuff You Need:

½ cup mashed bananas

1 tsp. lemon juice

½ cup butter, softened

3½ cups sifted confectioners' sugar

¾ cup light cream cheese

Hit It:

Mix the bananas and lemon juice together. Beat the butter and cream cheese until creamy. Alternate adding the sugar and banana, a small amount at a time; beat until light and fluffy. This makes enough frosting for the top and sides of one loaf of bread.

14-Karat Gold Mini Carrot Cakes
(with Praline-Cream Cheese Frosting)

Stuff You Need:

2 cups granulated sugar

1⅓ cups vegetable oil

3 large eggs (at room temp.)

1 tsp. vanilla extract

2 cups plus 1 Tbsp. flour, separated

2 tsp. baking soda

2 tsp. cinnamon

1½ tsp. salt

1 lb. carrots, grated

1 cup raisins

1 cup pecans, chopped

Hit It:

Preheat oven to 400°. Grease muffin pans or line them with paper muffin cups. In a large bowl, beat the sugar, oil, and eggs until light yellow; add the vanilla. In a separate bowl, sift together 2 cups of the flour with the baking soda, salt, and cinnamon; add to the wet ingredients. Toss the pecans, carrots, and raisins with the remaining Tbsp. of flour; add to the batter and mix well. Divide the batter among 22 muffin cups so that each is ¾ full. (**Tip:** Use an ice-cream scooper.) Bake for 10 minutes, then reduce oven to 350° and bake for 35 minutes or until a toothpick inserted into the center of the cakes comes out clean. Cool on a wire rack.

Makes 22 cakes.

Cream Cheese Frosting

Stuff You Need:

12 oz. cream cheese (at room temp.)

8 oz. unsalted butter (at room temp.)

1 tsp. vanilla extract

1 Tbsp. Grand Marnier or orange-
flavored liqueur (optional)

16 oz. confectioners' sugar, sifted
(**Huh?** Put through a small-mesh sieve and "tap through" until there are no lumps.)

¼ tsp. lemon juice

Hit It:

Mix the cream cheese, butter, vanilla, lemon juice, and Grand Marnier (if you want) together in a bowl until just incorporated; add the confectioners' sugar and mix until smooth. Frost each cake generously. (Do not frost your own tongue—you need the stuff for the cakes.) Prepare the pralines (below) and let them cool before placing them on top of the frosted carrot cakes.

Makes enough frosting for 22 cakes.

Praline Topping

Stuff You Need:

6 Tbsp. unsalted butter

1 cup light brown sugar

½ cup milk

½ cup maple syrup

¼ cup heavy cream

1 Tbsp. vanilla extract

1 cup pecans, broken up

Hit It:

Melt the butter in a skillet; add the sugar, milk, cream, maple syrup, and pecans and cook, stirring constantly, for 10 minutes at a rolling boil. Add the vanilla and cook, stirring constantly, until the mixture forms a string when you drag the spoon to the side of the pan. (This should take about 4–5 minutes.) Immediately spoon the pralines, about a tablespoon at a time, onto wax paper placed on a cookie sheet. Allow them to cool before placing on top of the frosted cakes.

Makes about 2 dozen pralines.

Dump Cake

One of my favorite food groups in high school was the one I called "cake with frosting." I figured that nothing could be better than making a cake from scratch, plus then I could control the "inch factor." Since supermarkets often only give you that measly ¼" of frosting, I thought it was a complete rip-off. So, armed with a box of cake mix and a huge can of frosting, I set out to make dessert history.

There were only two glitches: (1) I ate the unbaked cake mix from the bowl—almost all of it. (2) For my second course, I frosted my own tongue. It wasn't fair to the cake, but I was selfish in those days—what can I say? Now I spread the wealth.

When my good friend Katrina made this for me one day at her house, I practically lost it. In fact, Katrina, her dear husband, Marty, and I did a jig in the kitchen. And no one does a jig like Marty—he's hilarious.

Stuff You Need:

1 pkg. chocolate-cake
   mix with pudding

1 cup melted butter

1 can cherry pie filling

1 can crushed pineapple
   in syrup

Hit It:

Preheat oven to 350°. Then, just like the title says, dump the pineapple into a 13" x 9" baking pan and dump the cherry pie filling over that. Don't stir anything—honestly, you're just supposed to dump it all in the pan. Now dump the cake mix on top of the fruit and pour the melted butter evenly over that and bake for an hour. Finally, call 911—it's that good.

Serves 8.

Whine Cake

This cake is so delicious, it's not even real. It's unlike any flavor of cake I've ever tasted, since it has a hint of wine (believe it or not). When Katrina made it for my 2002 Christmas party, everyone flipped out. It's so flavorful and there's no butter in it . . . at least that's something.

Anyway, this recipe had to go in my book or I would have started whining.

Stuff You Need:

1 pkg. yellow-cake mix

1 small pkg. instant French-
   vanilla pudding mix

1 cup vegetable oil

1 cup sherry (not cooking sherry)

¼ tsp. nutmeg

3 eggs plus 2 egg yolks

½ cup walnuts, chopped (optional)

Powdered sugar (optional)

Hit It:

Preheat oven to 350°. Spray a Bundt pan with Pam and lightly flour it. Mix the cake mix, pudding mix, oil, sherry, and nutmeg until blended. Add the eggs and yolks, one at a time; beat on a low speed until just combined with no yolks visible. Fold in the nuts and pour the batter into a prepared pan. Put in the middle of the oven and bake for 50 minutes. Remove from the oven and let sit for 5 minutes. Invert the pan onto a pretty serving plate.

Serves 8–10.

Now Serving:

Dust on top with powdered sugar. You'll be whining for more of this cake after one slice!

Feeling Saucy Applesauce Cake
(with Get-Out-of-Here Brown-Sugar Frosting)

Here's a cake made with no eggs. Go figure! Yet it's sinfully good and majorly moist. Try to keep it to one piece, my friends.

Stuff You Need:

2 sticks unsalted butter, softened

2 cups superfine sugar

2 cups unsweetened applesauce (try to find a good-quality one)

3 cups all-purpose flour, sifted

1 cup pecans, chopped

1 cup raisins (light or dark or combo)

1 tsp. ground cinnamon

½ tsp. ground mace

¾ tsp. ground nutmeg

1¾ tsp. baking soda

1¼ tsp. vanilla extract
(**Tip:** Always use the best-quality one. It really makes a difference.)

Hit It:

Preheat oven to 325°. Butter a 9″ nonstick tube pan. (**Huh?** This is like a Bundt-cake pan, but without the ridges.) Dust with flour and shake off the excess. In a large mixing bowl, cream the butter and sugar until light and fluffy, about 2–3 minutes. Take a look at this mixture—isn't it pretty? Okay, get back to work by folding in the applesauce.

Dredge the raisins and nuts in ¼ cup of the flour mixture; sift together the remaining 2¾ cups of flour with the spices and baking soda. (**Tip:** When you're sifting, put the flour into a sifter and turn the handle . . . I know it's not exactly brain surgery. If you don't have a sifter, put through a small-mesh sieve and "tap through" until there are no lumps. You might have to do this in two batches.) Fold the dry flour mixture into the fluffy, creamy mixture and then add the vanilla, along with the nuts and raisins.

Pour the batter into the tube pan and bake for 1½ hours or until a knife inserted comes out clean. Cool and then invert onto a cake plate or serving platter. Prepare to get frosty with it.

Get-Out-of-Here Brown-Sugar Frosting

Stuff You Need:

2 cups light brown sugar, packed firmly

6 Tbsp. heavy cream

½ stick unsalted butter

1 tsp. vanilla extract

1 cup confectioners' sugar

1 Tbsp. cream cheese

Hit It:

Place all the ingredients, except the confectioners' sugar and vanilla, into a large saucepan and slowly bring to a rolling boil over a medium heat, stirring constantly. Remove from heat and stir in the vanilla and then the confectioners' sugar.

When the cake is cool, pour the frosting over the cake and let it drip down the sides. It'll set quickly, so don't spread it. Just let it flow down the sides by itself—it will look beautifully homemade.

Now Serving:

Get out the pretty plates for this one. It serves 10–14 (depending on how much dinner you ate).

Add a Pound of Butter Cake
(Butter-Toffee Pound Cake . . . Please Forgive Me)

Stuff You Need:

5 large eggs

3 cups all-purpose flour

2 cups light brown sugar, packed firmly

1 cup white sugar

1½ cups butter (at room temp.)

½ tsp. baking powder

½ tsp. salt

1 cup milk

1 tsp. vanilla extract

For the Icing:

1 lb. dark brown sugar

½ cup butter

½ cup heavy cream

A dash of salt

½ tsp. baking powder

½ tsp. vanilla extract

Hit It:

Preheat oven to 325°. Cream the brown sugar, white sugar, and butter with an electric mixer. Add eggs, one at a time, and beat only until incorporated. (**Tip:** Don't make the egg whites create any volume.) In a large bowl, sift together the flour, baking powder, and salt; add to the beaten batter alternately with milk, beginning and ending with the flour mixture. After each addition, beat at a low speed just until blended. Add the vanilla extract and pour the batter into a greased and floured Bundt pan.

Bake 70–80 minutes or until a toothpick inserted in the center comes out clean. Cool in the pan on a wire rack for 20 minutes; now make the icing.

In a medium saucepan, bring to a boil the butter, brown sugar, cream, and salt, stirring constantly for 4 minutes. Remove from heat; add the baking powder and vanilla. Beat with an electric mixer for 6 minutes, until icing becomes thick. Invert the pan to remove the cake and drizzle with the icing.

Serves 10.

Now Serving:

This also makes a fabulous brunch dessert.

Everybody Was Tofu Biting
(Sugar-Free Tofu-Chocolate Mousse)

Praise the Lord—a dessert that's all protein __and__ sugar free! This is also a great one for gastric-bypass patients.

Stuff You Need:

1 lb. soft, silken tofu

6 oz. good unsweetened baking chocolate (such as the kind made by Valrhona or Scharffen Berger), not cocoa powder— this is the "bar" type chocolate

1 cup Splenda or Equal, granulated (**Tip:** Make sure that you're using a sweetener that measures the same as sugar, cup for cup.)

½ cup whipping cream, divided in two

A dash of salt

2 tsp. pure vanilla

Hit It:

Blend the tofu, sweetener, salt, and vanilla until smooth and creamy. Melt the chocolate and ¼ cup of the whipping cream over low heat; gradually blend into the tofu mixture and allow to cool. In a separate chilled bowl, beat the other ¼ cup cream until stiff peaks form. Fold gently into the chocolate-tofu mixture until incorporated. Pour into individual serving dishes and chill.

Makes 6 half-cup servings.

A Delicious Variation:

Take 1 cup frozen unsweetened raspberries and defrost completely. Using the back of a wooden spoon, press the berries through a fine strainer or sieve to remove the seeds. Sweeten the resulting raspberry puree with ¼ cup sweetener. Add the puree to the tofu-chocolate mixture immediately before the whipped cream is added.

Carnie Aside-a:

For a fluffier version that's not as dense, add 1 box sugar-free chocolate pudding mix, made according to the directions on the box with 1% milk (it doesn't matter if you've added the raspberries). Before the pudding sets, fold into the tofu mixture before adding the melted chocolate. This will increase the number of portions by 4–6.

153

Sharon's Black Forest Cookie Surprises

My great friend Jack Kugell requests these babies once a year for his birthday. So his mom, Sharon, now just calls them "Jack's Birthday Cookies."

By the way, the surprise in these cookies is in the toppings. These babies are just too good to be true and make a perfect holiday gift. I swear, Sharon should open her own bakery. She's one of the best cooks and bakers I know, and I love her and Bube (my special name for Jack) with all my heart.

Stuff You Need:

½ cup butter or margarine

1 cup plus 2 tsp. sugar

1 extra-large egg

1½ cups flour

½ cup unsweetened cocoa

⅓ tsp. baking powder

¼ tsp. baking soda

A pinch of salt

1⅔ tsp. vanilla

For the Topping:

16-oz. jar maraschino cherries, reserving
    2 tsp. juice (**Tip:** Try to resist eating
    them before you make the cookies.)

7 oz. semisweet chocolate morsels
    (**Tip:** See above tip.)

½ cup condensed milk

⅛ tsp. salt

Hit It:

Preheat oven to 350°. Mix the butter, sugar, egg, and vanilla together until fluffy. In another bowl, mix all the dry ingredients together; gradually blend them into the butter mixture. Form the dough into a large ball, wrap it tightly in plastic wrap, and place it in the fridge for at least an hour. (When the dough is cold, it will be easy to handle.) Make 1" dough balls, and place on an ungreased cookie sheet. Drain the cherries and save the juice. Place one cherry on top of each ball and gently push it halfway into the dough. Set aside while preparing the topping.

Place the chocolate pieces, condensed milk, and salt in a double boiler (you can also use a heavy medium saucepan) over medium-low heat until mixture starts to melt. Mix together until the chocolate is smooth; add the cherry juice and stir to give the mixture a gloss. Using a teaspoon, swirl the chocolate around each cherry until the cherry is totally covered but the cookie isn't. Bake 10–12 minutes. Allow the cookies to cool before removing them from the cookie sheet.

Makes about 26–30 yummy cookies.

Hula Heck Thought of This?
Hawaiian Lu-*ahh* Sundaes

Stuff You Need:

1 cup pineapple chunks, fresh or canned (if you must), reserving 2 Tbsp. juice

2 large, ripe bananas, sliced into ½″ circles

¼ cup butter (½ stick)

¼ cup brown sugar

2 Tbsp. coconut rum (I like Malibu brand)

4–6 scoops of your favorite vanilla ice cream (try McConnell's Vanilla Bean—there should be a law . . .)

Hit It:

In a heavy skillet, melt the butter; when it's sizzling but not brown, add the sugar. Stir to caramelize, about 2 minutes. Gently add the pineapple, juice, and bananas and continue to cook until warmed through.

Splash on the rum. (**Huge Tip:** Be careful! It may ignite.) Allow to cook for an additional minute or until the alcohol burns off. Immediately spoon over the ice cream that you've scooped into wide dessert or sundae dishes—and get me a muzzle before I eat it all!

Serves 4–6.

I Scream for Fruit Ice Cream

Stuff You Need:

1 lb. frozen fruit (strawberries, peaches, mangoes, blueberries, or any combination)

2 individual containers (6–8 oz. each) light (using non-sugar sweetener) custard-style yogurt, vanilla or any fruit flavor

2 Tbsp. Splenda or Equal, or sweeten to taste

Hit It:

(**Tip:** The fruit must be frozen solid and the yogurt refrigerated.) Place the fruit, a cup at a time, into a food processor and pulse (blend lightly) for 5–10 seconds after each addition. Add 1 container of yogurt and the sweetener and blend for 30 seconds or so, until the fruit chunks are gone but the mixture is still frozen. Keep adding spoons of the second container of yogurt until an ice-cream-like consistency is achieved—that is, it's thick enough to hold its shape when spooned into dishes or cones. Taste for sweetness and add more sweetener if desired. (**Tip:** This should be eaten immediately, as the texture will become too hard to scoop if refrozen.)

Serves 4–6.

Guilt-Free Let It Snow Cones

I thought I'd end this chapter with a note from my good friend Katrina:

Ah, childhood. I remember when it was 100-plus degrees in California, I'd use snow cones to satisfy my craving for cool. In fact, I became so addicted that I even bought a Hawaiian-shaved-ice machine and went pro.

These days both the ice shavers (only $20–$60) and the really interesting syrups are available at stores and on the Internet. I just bought a new machine at Target and I love it. It's an instant rewind back to the days when my biggest worry was if I should use coconut or mango syrup.

One quick tip: Try to get a machine that takes regular ice cubes rather than having to use ice that must be frozen in special molds, which is a minor pain.

Now get out your machines and let it snow, let it snow, let it snow.

Love,
Kat

Stuff You Need:

1 tray ice cubes (or ice frozen in molds that are custom made for an ice shaver)

Any flavor Torani, DaVinci, or Monin syrup (**Tip:** These are usually found in the coffee section of the market, or sometimes in import stores in larger bottles. Every flavor is good, but nothing is as good as the Torani hazelnut syrup. Tied for a close second are raspberry, chocolate, Irish cream, vanilla, and mint. And if you want to go skinny, try one of the yummy sugar-free syrups on the market.)

Hit It:

You'll need an ice shaver of some sort (HawaiIce makes my favorite). An old-fashioned hand-cranked one will also do, and it will be a major hit with company.

You may put the "snow" into paper cups, paper cones, or just tall glasses and drizzle syrup over the top.

Carnie Aside-a:

If you use sugar-free syrups, then this dessert is a freebie calorie-wise and will also boost your water intake. Six months after my gastric-bypass surgery, I started to crave sugar, and this was my favorite dessert at night while watching TV. It really hits the spot.

AFTERWORD

Well Done—
a Final Note

Well, there you have it: My first cookbook, and I hope there will be many more to come.

So what's the worst thing that could happen if you make the dishes I've just shared with you: You either poison your guests or burn down the house? Ha ha! No, it's all in good fun. Just enjoy yourself and remember that there's nothing like serving *something* you love to *someone* you love.

Bon appétit! Oh, and save a bite for me.

APPENDIX

Tipping
the Scales

Excuse me for one moment because I'm in the middle of sampling some homemade whipped cream I'm using in a dessert. After tasting it (you know I'm doing this for you), a thought went through my mind: *Maybe we should talk about cutting calories for a second.*

It's great to cook the real thing with all the calories and just eat smaller portions—that's what I've been doing ever since having gastric-bypass surgery years ago and it works. But there are also times when I want to drop a quick ten pounds—yet I still don't want to totally deny myself. So how can we lighten up with style and great taste? Experiment with the following choices. (**Note:** Just because I've given you these substitutions doesn't mean that they always work. It's all about experimenting to find the taste you love.)

Instead of:	Use:
1 cup butter in baking	1 cup applesauce
8 oz. cream cheese	8 oz. yogurt cheese
1 cup crème fraîche	1 cup yogurt cheese
1 cup heavy cream (in recipes, not whipping)	2 tsp. cornstarch or 1 Tbsp. flour whisked into 1 cup nonfat milk
1 cup sour cream	1 cup low-fat cottage cheese with 2 Tbsp. skim milk and 1 Tbsp. lemon juice
1 cup fat for sautéing	4 cups low-fat stock, fruit juice, or wine; sauté until liquid evaporates
1 egg	2 egg whites
1 cup oil or fat for basting	1 cup fruit juice or 1 cup low-fat stock

If you want to pass on:	Sub in:
Bacon	Turkey bacon or lean ham
Basting with butter	Wine, fruit juice, or bouillon
Butter	Reduced-calorie margarine; safflower, soybean, corn, canola, or peanut oil
Chocolate, unsweetened (1 oz.)	3 Tbsp. unsweetened cocoa plus 1 Tbsp. margarine
Cream cheese	Nonfat or light-process cream cheese; Neufchâtel cheese
Cream soup (added into recipe)	Pureed, cooked potato
Cream	Evaporated skim milk
Egg (1)	¼ cup egg substitute or 2 egg whites
Frosting	Dust a cake with cinnamon, cocoa, or confectioners' sugar
Fudge sauce	Low-fat chocolate syrup
Ground beef	Ground turkey
Mayonnaise	Low-fat or fat-free mayo; whipped salad dressing; plain yogurt combined with equal part low-fat cottage cheese
Oil (for baking)	Applesauce
Ricotta cheese	Low-fat or fat-free cottage cheese; nonfat or low-fat ricotta
Salad dressing	Follow the directions on a Good Seasonings packet, but use nonfat yogurt instead of oil
Sausage	Lean ground beef; 95% fat-free sausage
Shortening	Soybean, corn, canola, or peanut oil in amount reduced by ⅓
Sour cream	Plain yogurt or ½ cup cottage cheese blended with 1¼ tsp. lemon juice; or fat-free sour cream
Whipped cream	Whipped evaporated skim milk (chill before whipping)

For My Gastric-Bypass Friends

What? Did you think I forgot about you? There's no way I could ever write a cookbook without you in mind. Don't forget that I will *always* be a gastric-bypass (GB) patient, too.

I'm five years post-op now and living a very healthy, normal lifestyle. I'm not afraid of food, and I shouldn't be. The difference now is that I control my portions.

My experience with eating over the last five years has changed dramatically. The first year I'd never dream of eating more than a teeny bite of a brownie, but now I'm able to have two or three bites, or a very small piece if I haven't overeaten with my dinner. Another difference is that I eat something like this as a dessert and not a snack.

The key to maintenance is balance and remembering calories in versus calories out (or how many you burn on a daily basis). If I do splurge a little bit, then I need to be accountable for those calories. That's where an extra half-hour walk comes in, or I drink more water.

There's a rule I always follow when I eat my meals: I have my protein first. This is great advice that you can take with you for the rest of your life because it enables you to eat whatever you want. You'll just be eating more of the protein—and filling up on it—and less of the carbs. But you still get to enjoy it all!

Every GB patient's tolerance for specific foods varies. Some people can't tolerate sugar, higher-fat-content foods, nuts, or certain meats at all. It's important that you're not afraid of your new possible limitations; instead, see what works for you, what makes you feel good, and what you enjoy eating. You'll be surprised by how things will change over the years.

There's no reason on Earth why you shouldn't be able to enjoy all types of wonderful food. Just go at your own pace, and respect and honor your limitations.

Here are a few other tips:

♥ Always eat slowly. Take little bites and chew thoroughly.

♥ As I mentioned above, hands down, the most important thing with any meal is that you must eat your protein first. This is the best advice I can give a GB patient. Protein fills you up and keeps you satisfied longer. End of story.

♥ Snacking is a no-no because it's more calories that will add up during the day, and it constantly pushes and stretches at the *anastomosis* (the connection between the stomach and the intestine that keeps you feeling full). You don't want to stretch it out— you want it to stay tight so that food stays in your pouch. That way you'll feel full by basically eating less food.

♥ Never drink liquids with your meals (or a half hour before or after). There's a reason for this: You don't want to fill up before a meal or flush the food out of your pouch while you're eating (enabling you to eat more food). Instead, you'll want to keep that food in your belly to help you stay satisfied longer.

♥ Remember the ultimate key: *tiny bites and tiny portions.*

THERE ARE PLENTY OF "CLEANER" RECIPES in this book that I recommend for you that follow all these rules. Let's start at the beginning. . . .

Breakfasts: Why not try **Egging You on Omelettes?** They're the perfect protein breakfast. So is **You'll Always Remember Your First Quiche. A Perfect Parfait** with nonfat yogurt made with Splenda is great, but skip the granola. On a weekend or for brunch make the **You Say Potato, I Say Frittata** or **Brunch Pie, Oh My!** I try not to eat carbs for breakfast and save them for lunch or dinner, but it's your call.

Lunches: Sometimes GB patients aren't even hungry for lunch. Not me, honey—I need three meals a day! Yet in your first few months out of surgery, it's possible that you'll be eating a piece of string cheese and a couple of apple slices as a meal because it fills you up. Don't get frustrated with it, but try to be creative. Perhaps you'll eventually be able to eat one egg, a little bit of cottage cheese, and a bite of fruit for lunch, or even a half cup of soup. You might also still be comfortable with cottage cheese and applesauce as a meal. Be sure to check with your surgeon's program and pay attention to the guidelines given to you. Know that different foods will slowly be added to your life.

For those of you who can handle a little more food, there are perfect lunches in this book that are satisfying and will hold you over until dinner. An **I Can Name That Tuna . . . Salad** is fine served with half of a sliced apple. I'm also partial to the **Viva Las Veggies Mexican Salad** because you get your veggies in. **Burger Queen** is fabulous, but you should omit the bun and add some sliced tomatoes and a scoop of cottage cheese (or have only half of the bun). **Rob's Mom's Split-Pea Soup** is another great choice. A few times a week you can even go **Loco for Quesadillas.**

Appetizers: They're generally a no-no unless you only have a couple of bites before you eat your meal—this goes along with the no-snacking rule. Also, make sure that your meals are eaten within 20 minutes, and keep in mind that we fill up quickly. At a party, a perfect appetizer for me to eat is a shrimp cocktail (but just one or two pieces) or a cube of cheese. But if you know your limitations, fill up on that protein first, whether it's in an appetizer or dinner form. The appetizers from this book I recommend are **How Swedish It Is Meatballs,**

Chicken Wings for My Sweetie (but be careful if you're sensitive to honey—sometimes I dump from it), **Olé Soufflés, Tuna Tartare,** and **Curried-Away Tofu Dip** (with veggies only).

Dinner: Any of the dinners in this book would be a perfect choice for GB patients (except for the lasagna, mac and cheese, or **Tuna Canoodle**) because their main focus is protein. However, the cleanest dinners I can recommend are **Poached Salmon with Unforgetta Bruschetta, Give Your Company the Bird, Perfect Breasts and Thighs, Miso Hungry,** and **Yeah, It's Oy Vey Brisket.** As for the lasagna, mac and cheese, and **Tuna Canoodle,** I'd think of them as pasta dishes: They're filling and you won't get enough protein. They're just not the best choice for a meal, but don't get sad. You have plenty to choose from, and this doesn't mean that you can't have a few bites.

Side Dishes: Watch it, watch it, watch it! You can make an exception for the **That's Amore** Italian veggies; the **Broiled Tomatoes; Great Greek-Style Beans; A Hill of Beans; Oh, Baby Carrots;** and **Ro-Ro-Roast Your Veggies.** I don't mean to say that you can't have the other sides, but most of them are rich and should be eaten in very small portions—even though they're my absolute favorites. This is always a challenge for me, and no one is perfect.

Desserts: What can I say? I'm sorry, you can't have any. Just kidding! The most important thing to remember is that dessert can make you feel sick because of the sugar content. Make sure to have a bite or two immediately following your meal if you choose to indulge. (That would be me—I'm not into deprivation.) The best choices in this book for GB patients are the **Guilt-Free Let It Snow Cones, I Scream for Fruit Ice Cream,** and **Everybody Was Tofu Biting.** Guidelines for all the other desserts are the following: one to three small bites and then stop, pour salt on the rest, give it to somebody else, feed it to your dog or your mate, but most important—get that dessert out of your sight. If you forget about it, the feeling of wanting it will pass quickly. See, you've got to enjoy yourself and have some, but you're not pigging out on two or three portions of it. Isn't that empowering?

This is where my gratitude sets in. God bless my little pouch and the fact that I'm going to "dump" (when too much sugar is "dumped" into your small intestine) if I eat more. I simply close my eyes and know that I'm lucky to have dessert in the first place. What a difference from how I used to feel! This is where my newfound appreciation for food comes into play, too.

I CAN'T LIE, THOUGH: Once in a while, I get a feeling of, *Why can't I have more? Oh God, it tastes so good . . . I just want one more bite. . . .*

That's when I rely on willpower and the ability to stand up and walk away. I know you can do it, too. Remember, nothing tastes as good as the feeling of being thin and healthy. And why would I want to dump, feel sick, and have to lie down in the other room? What an embarrassment!

By the way, GB friends, your own personal cookbook is simmering right now. I hope to serve it to you soon—after all, we're in this together! Good luck . . . and I'm so proud of you.

Love,
Carnie

A Helping
of Thanks

To Cindy: You're my friend and my wonderful writing partner. This was a total blast! You're very talented, and I'm so grateful that we're connected in such a special way. Can't wait for more . . . love you.

To my husband, Rob: You're my baby doll, and I love you more than anything in the world. Thanks for testing the food all these years, my Hony (this goes for the dogs, too!).

To Katrina (Aney): You're a very special person, *and* you're also the best cook I know! We had so much fun, didn't we? Thank you for your amazing recipes and for all your help, passion, devotion, and most of all, friendship. *I love you. Love, Stainy*

Thanks also to: Mickey Shapiro (I thank God for you every day); Pam Miller (your love and advice is "priceless"); Daniel (my stepfather), Melinda, Daria, Delanie, Dylan, Gloria, Wendy, Dan, Leo, Beau, Zoe, Noah, Dee-Dee, Tiffany, Barb, Chris, Sky, and all my family and friends (I wish I could mention you all, but you know who you are and I love you dearly).

To Hay House: for partnering with me once again!

To Martin Mann: for the awesome photos of the food in this book.

And to the people who contributed their wonderful recipes, thank you for sharing: Katrina Zucker, Mae Rovell, Marilyn Wilson, Lynn Wasser, Grandma Betty and the McKays, Owen Elliot Kugell, Sharon Doernberg, Daniel Combs, Gloria Felix, Maureen Reicher, Renee Pearlman (you'd be proud!), Vasili Scandalis and Anna (Maria!), Marti and Robin Spector, and Bonnie Auerbach.

One more thank you (does it ever end?): to Paula Deen, Emeril Lagasse, and Ina Garten—you might not know it, but you inspire and motivate me to be a better cook. You all rule!

Last, but not least, to Lola: You were in my tummy as I wrote this book. Your daddy and I love you more than anything in the world. You were made out of love, which is the best recipe of all. Always remember that you are our precious little girl.

♥ ♥ ♥

About
Carnie Wilson

Carnie Wilson is an actress, voice-over artist, singer, motivator, and mother. She shares her personal story and helps educate people about morbid obesity during the lectures she presents throughout the U.S. Carnie lives with her musician husband, Rob, and their three adorable dogs in Los Angeles. She is also the author of *Gut Feelings* and *I'm Still Hungry* (the latter with Cindy Pearlman).

About
Cindy Pearlman

Cindy Pearlman is a nationally syndicated writer for the *New York Times Syndicate* and the *Chicago Sun-Times*. Her work has appeared in *Entertainment Weekly, Premiere, People, Ladies' Home Journal, McCall's, Seventeen, Movieline,* and *Cinescape.* Over the past 15 years, she has interviewed Hollywood's biggest stars, who appear in her column "The Big Picture." Cindy is also the co-author of numerous books.

Cover and Food Photos: Martin Mann
www.martinmann.com
www.nimagazine.com

Food Stylists: The Clever Cleaver Brothers®:
Steve Cassarino and Lee N. Gerovitz

The Clever Cleaver Brothers® are cookbook authors,
magazine columnists, DVD/video producers, and hosts of **www.clevercleaver.com**.
For more information, please e-mail the Clever Cleaver Brothers® at **scassarino@aol.com**.

Cooking Notes

Cooking Notes

Cooking Notes

Cooking Notes

Cooking Notes

Cooking Notes

Cooking Notes

♥ ♥ ♥

We hope you enjoyed this Hay House Lifestyles cookbook.
If you'd like to receive a free catalog featuring additional
Hay House books and products, or if you'd like information
about the Hay Foundation, please contact:

Hay House, Inc.
P.O. Box 5100
Carlsbad, CA 92018-5100

(760) 431-7695 or **(800) 654-5126**
(760) 431-6948 (fax) or **(800) 650-5115 (fax)**
www.hayhouse.com

♥ ♥ ♥

Published and distributed in Australia by:
Hay House Australia Pty. Ltd. • 18/36 Ralph St.
• Alexandria NSW 2015 • *Phone:* 612-9669-4299
• *Fax:* 612-9669-4144 • www.hayhouse.com.au

Published and distributed in the United Kingdom by:
Hay House UK, Ltd. • Unit 62, Canalot Studios •
222 Kensal Rd., London W10 5BN • *Phone:* 44-20-8962-1230
• *Fax:* 44-20-8962-1239 • www.hayhouse.co.uk

Published and distributed in the Republic of South Africa by:
Hay House SA (Pty), Ltd., P.O. Box 990, Witkoppen 2068
• *Phone/Fax:* 27-11-706-6612 •
orders@psdprom.co.za

Distributed in Canada by:
Raincoast • 9050 Shaughnessy St., Vancouver, B.C. V6P 6E5 •
Phone: (604) 323-7100 • *Fax:* (604) 323-2600

♥ ♥ ♥

Tune in to **www.hayhouseradio.com**™ for the best in inspirational talk radio
featuring top Hay House authors! And, sign up via the Hay House USA Website to receive
the Hay House online newsletter and stay informed about what's going on with your favorite
authors. You'll receive bimonthly announcements about: Discounts and Offers, Special Events,
Product Highlights, Free Excerpts, Giveaways, and more!
www.hayhouse.com